Nostalgic Memories
of
MANCHESTER

NOSTALGIC MEMORIES OF MANCHESTER

The publishers would like to thank the following companies for their

support in the production of this book

F Duerr & Sons Ltd

Elcometer Ltd

Joseph Gleave & Son Ltd

Glendale Foods

ITAC Limited

JW Lees

Manchester Arndale

Manchester High School for Girls

The Morson Group

Procter & Gamble

Renolds Plc

RRG Group

Searchlight

Stax

Sykes Seafood

Waters MS Technologies Centre/Micromass UK Ltd

William Hulme's Grammar School

Withington Girls' School

First published in Great Britain by True North Books Limited
England HX3 6SN
01422 244555
www.truenorthbooks.com

ISBN 978 - 1906649746

Text, design and origination by True North Books
Printed and bound by The Amadeus Press

Nostalgic Memories
of
MANCHESTER

CONTENTS

INTRODUCTION

Such has been the popularity of our previous books on the Manchester area, that we have been encouraged to produce a new publication. Our books allow readers to walk on cobbled streets, browse in well known local shops of the period and revisit special events and occasions, without leaving the comfort of their favourite armchair.

Change is relentless and in some parts of the area the transformation will be more obvious than others. Manchester's city centre and the roads around it have changed significantly from times gone by. Some of the older and architecturally impressive buildings have retained their originality on the outside, although their uses have changed. The title of this new book, 'Nostalgic Memories of Manchester', tells you all you need to know about what is captured within its covers.

Turning over the pages will bring you to a treasure trove from the last century. Through the photographs, images and thoughtful text, the reader is taken on a steam train ride back through the mists of time to an age when mum would nip into J Lyons and Co for afternoon tea and dad could buy a suit at the Fifty Shilling Tailor. We make no apologies for the fact that some of the photographs will be outside living memory because they will still be familiar to us. They may feature an event described to us by a close relative or they could feature historical landmarks such as monuments and buildings.

The companies and organisations that have thrived in the area, over the recent decades, are many. The Greater Manchester district has a proud tradition of creativity, enterprise and innovation and we take great pleasure in including in this book, histories of an outstanding selection of different companies, whose contribution to the development and sustainability of the city's economic prosperity is a matter of record. With their co-operation and access to their respective photographic archives, we have been able to tell their stories. Hopefully this will trigger the memories of local people who have worked for them, or been touched by their part in community life.

Whatever the view taken on the boundaries which separate 'history', 'nostalgia' or 'the present', we should all invest a little time occasionally to reflect on the past and the people and events which helped to shape life as we know it today.

CONCILIO ET LABORE

TEXT	ANDREW MITCHELL, STEVE AINSWORTH, TONY LAX
PHOTOGRAPH RESEARCH	TONY LAX
DESIGNER	SEAMUS MOLLOY
BUSINESS DEVELOPMENT MANAGER	PETER PREST

VICTORIAN MANCHESTER

By the time Victoria ascended the throne in 1837, Manchester was established as one of the world's leading industrial centres. During her reign it would continue to grow at a rapid rate and become known as 'Cottonopolis', the hub of a massive market for cotton goods.

The number of mills reached a peak in 1853, the year in which it was granted city status. But, all this came at a price. The wealth that was created lay in the hands of the few. Mill owners, railway bosses and those running engineering companies dwelt in fine mansions, employed large staffs of servants and enjoyed

all manner of home comforts. A large portion of the lower ranks, who worked to provide the middle and upper classes with their prosperity, lived in poverty and degrading conditions. Low wages, long hours, dangerous working conditions and poor domestic sanitation offered a bleak existence. Infant mortality was shockingly high and those who survived cholera epidemics, the ravages of scarlet fever and the scourges of diarrhoea were expected to join their parents on the workplace floor at a very early age. Factory chimneys and domestic flues belched out palls of smoke that hung over the city, ensuring that respiratory disease was commonplace. Even by the end of the 19th century, life expectancy was just 45; less for those from the underclasses. By then, a better social conscience was coming to the fore. The 1870 Education Act provided elementary schooling for the masses, housing reforms were introduced and new sewers built. Social attitudes were changing, albeit slowly.

Left: Oldham Street links the A665 Great Ancoats Street and A6 Oldham Road with Piccadilly. It is not as upmarket a retail area as it was in the early 1900s. Along here, at the junction with Dale Street, Affleck and Brown's independent department store, known by some as the 'Harrods of the North', had built a fine reputation based on a first class service. We can tell that this was a shopping area that attracted those with some degree of standing. Just look at the delightful dresses and hats sported by the women we can see. You did not get to wear such finery if your day job was in a mill or down at the laundry.

Above: East Didsbury's Ye Olde Cock Inn took its name from the dubious practice of cockfighting once common here. The blood sport was associated with heavy betting and attracted spectators from all walks of life. It became illegal in England in 1835. Situated at 848 Wilmslow Road, close to the old village green, the pub has much the same appearance as it did 150 years ago, from which time this peaceful scene was captured. The building to its right now contains the Didsbury Village Restaurant.

Left: Manchester has long had an interest in classical music. As far back as 1848, Charles Hallé (1819-95), a German pianist, settled in Manchester and established a series of concerts. He set up the orchestra that would bear his name in 1857, soon finding a home at the Free Trade Hall. This image shows the Russian violinist Adolph Brodsky (1851-1929) and his wife, Anna, about the time of their marriage in 1880. To the right are Edvard Hagerup Grieg (1843-1907), the Norwegian composer of 'Peer Gynt' and his wife, Nina. At the invitation of Hallé, Brodsky came to Manchester to direct the orchestra and teach at the Royal Manchester College of Music, becoming its principal in 1896 and making the city his home.

Bottom left: By the 1840s, baby carriages were becoming extremely popular and at the very top of upper class life. It is reported that, even Queen Victoria bought three carriages from Hitchings Baby Store. The carriages of those days were built of wood or wicker and held together by expensive brass joints.

These sometimes became heavily ornamented works of art. Models were also named after royalty, Princess and Duchess being popular names, as well as Balmoral and Windsor. In this rare photograph we see a young child looking out from a large pram which could have been based upon a Lines Brothers model of the time. The horses bob up and down as the pram moves forwards. It was possibly built around 1887 to coincide with Queen Victoria's Golden Jubilee.

Below: The late 19th century stalls were situated on either side of Market Place. At the time, they were particularly noted for the sale of flowers, fruit, vegetables and poultry. The roof of the Old Wellington pub can be seen sticking out beyond the building on the corner. It was the first in a row of medieval buildings in a part of the city known as The Shambles. Looking north, away from the city, the building in the centre belonged to G and W Yates, seedsmen and florists. To its right was the Sir John Falstaff pub. This is roughly where Marks & Spencer stands today.

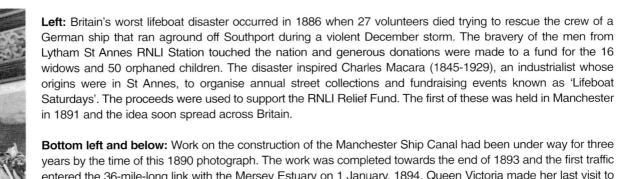

Left: Britain's worst lifeboat disaster occurred in 1886 when 27 volunteers died trying to rescue the crew of a German ship that ran aground off Southport during a violent December storm. The bravery of the men from Lytham St Annes RNLI Station touched the nation and generous donations were made to a fund for the 16 widows and 50 orphaned children. The disaster inspired Charles Macara (1845-1929), an industrialist whose origins were in St Annes, to organise annual street collections and fundraising events known as 'Lifeboat Saturdays'. The proceeds were used to support the RNLI Relief Fund. The first of these was held in Manchester in 1891 and the idea soon spread across Britain.

Bottom left and below: Work on the construction of the Manchester Ship Canal had been under way for three years by the time of this 1890 photograph. The work was completed towards the end of 1893 and the first traffic entered the 36-mile-long link with the Mersey Estuary on 1 January, 1894. Queen Victoria made her last visit to the city on 21 May of that year to perform the official opening ceremony. She also knighted the Mayors of Salford and Manchester, William Bailey and Anthony Marshall. The canal cost £15 million to build, but it made Manchester the third busiest port in Britain, despite its distance from the coast.

Running from the Eastham Locks in Liverpool to Salford Quays, the Manchester Ship Canal opened in 1894 as the longest navigable river canal in the world. It gave ocean going vessels access to the inland port, but never really gave its backers the financial returns for which they hoped. As the second half of the 20th century unfolded, the canal did not generate the level of business that had been anticipated and, as larger and larger vessels were built, it was just not big enough to serve the demands of modern shipping. Plans to make the Mersey navigable from its estuary to the Salford district were mooted as far back as the 17th century. The Mersey and Irwell Navigation Company succeeded in opening up the

waterway in the 1730s, but only for craft of limited tonnage. It fell into disrepair in the 1880s and the increase in taxes levied by the Port of Liverpool but the cost of conveying freight by rail made the building of the Ship Canal attractive. One of the main landmarks along its route is the swing aqueduct at Barton. The only one of its type in the world because of its swinging action, it allows narrowboats on the Bridgewater Canal to pass above large boats on the Ship Canal below. The eastern end of the canal has been redeveloped over the last 20 or more years for a mixture of business, residential and recreational facilities.

Below: What eventually became Piccadilly Gardens was formerly the site of Manchester Royal Infirmary. This part of the city centre was then known as Lever's Row. The Infirmary's history can be traced to the cottage hospital that was founded by Charles White in 1752 in Garden Street, near Withy Grove. It soon outgrew its premises and relocated in 1755. By the Edwardian era, those in charge of administration had become jumpy about fire safety. There had been several recent disastrous blazes in nearby buildings and evacuation of staff and patients in an overcrowded area might be a major problem if the Infirmary suffered a similar plight. The premises also required modernising, so it made sense to move on and in 1908 it relocated to Oxford Road.

Right: This is not the Victorian equivalent of Girls Aloud, but was a noisy set of women nonetheless. They had a mission and that was one of equality. Emmeline Pankhurst née Goulden (1858-1928), pictured with daughters Christabel and Sylvia, was a Moss Side girl. She was a member of the Women's Franchise League that promoted women's rights, but formed the Women's Political and Social Union in 1898, with particular reference to voting in political elections and dedicated to 'deeds not words'. Members became known as suffragettes and Pankhurst's voice was one of the loudest of them all. Women over 30 were granted the right to vote in 1918. This was extended in 1928 to those over 21, just a month after Emmeline's death.

Bottom right: Although from the 1890s, the Market Street scene, photographed near to Brown Street, has an almost Dickensian feel in terms of some of the fashion sense on display. The colours are dark and there is little in the way of the dandy or peacock strutting his stuff. There was some change on the way, though, in the styles that women favoured. Clothes became simpler and less fussy as crinolines and bustles fell from favour. Waists were more waspish and jackets cut with high collars. Most of the people we see are well turned out and it is evident that these locals belonged to a part of society that was comfortably off.

STREET SCENES

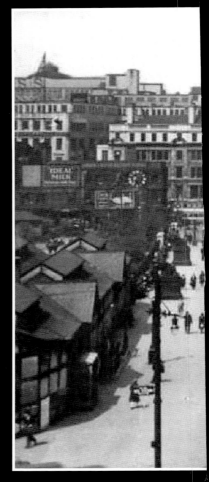

The earliest view of Piccadilly dates from towards the end of the Edwardian era. Running from the centre to the right, the names of Black and Green, the Redgrave Mill Company, Midland Railway and Chorlton Brothers mean little to most of us now, but they dominated this spot a century ago. The 1931 image shows how important this part of the city had become as a terminus for both buses and trams that ferried people in from the suburbs. Close to London Road Station, it was also handily placed at the top of Market Street. As traffic went past, Robert Peel (1788-1850) looked down on the scene from his plinth. He was a major political figure of the first half of the 19th century. Born in Bury, he became a Member of Parliament at the tender age of 21, rising to the dizzy height of Prime Minister on two separate occasions in the 1830s and 1840s. His statue was paid for by public subscription and sculpted by W Calder Marshall. It was unveiled on 12 October 1853. After the closure of the Infirmary in the early 1900s, a determined effort was made to turn Piccadilly Gardens into a green oasis in the heart of the city. Local inhabitants, especially office workers, looked forward to sunny lunchtimes spent idling away the time with a packet of sandwiches, a Thermos of tea and a Woodbine to finish off the occasion with a smoky flourish. During the last war air raid shelters were erected and the flower beds and lawns were dug up during the Dig for Victory campaign, but they regained much of their former glory in peacetime. The Gardens and square were revamped earlier this century. Building construction on the perimeter make them feel far less open than they used to seem.

Right: Michael Marks, an immigrant from Poland, ran modest market stalls in Leeds and the northwest before teaming up with a Skipton born cashier, Thomas Spencer to open a store on Cheetham Hill Road. Their cheap and cheerful goods, sold in Penny Bazaars, established the company that would become a High Street giant affectionately known as 'Marks & Sparks'. The shop on Oldham Street was photographed in 1908, by which time both the founders had died and the company was well established as a limited company.

Below: St Peter's Church, seen from Oxford Street in c1905, was soon to be no more. It was consecrated on 6 September, 1794, and stood on Mosley Street until it was demolished following the Churches Act of 1906 that merged this parish with several others. The land that was freed up was used as part of a street

widening exercise. In 1924, the War Memorial was erected approximately where St Peter's once stood. The Princes Theatre, to the left, opened on 15 October, 1864. It was then managed by Mrs Charles Calvert, formerly in charge of the Theatre Royal. The first production starred the Calverts as Prospero and Miranda in Shakespeare's 'The Tempest'. The Princes closed in 1940.

Below: Newgate, off Corporation Street, was a desperately poor part of Manchester in 1908. It was truly a slum area where the families had to endure the most primitive of living conditions. Forget all about electricity and modern plumbing, you would have been lucky to find running water. The toilet areas were outdoor privies and the cramped living conditions were a perfect breeding ground for disease. The homes were damp and TB, bronchitis and pneumonia all too commonplace. Nearly half the children did not survive the illnesses that beset them and perished before they reached the age of five. There were no good old days for the residents of Newgate.

The modest housing on Charles Street seemed to cower in the shadow of the imposing Refuge Assurance Building. This magnificent structure was one of Alfred Waterhouse's many designs and was erected on the corner of Oxford Street and Whitworth Street. The first phase of this red brick and terracotta structure was completed in 1895. Its ground floor was an impressive open hall that took your breath away as you passed through the portals. The marvellous 217 foot high tower was added during the extension work along Oxford Street that was completed in 1912, not long before the time that the dray horse and its barrels were pictured. This phase of the Refuge Assurance Building's development was overseen by Waterhouse's son, Paul. Stanley Birkett added to its growth in 1932. The Refuge occupied the site until 1987. It was converted into the Palace Hotel in 1996.

Kelsall's and the seed merchant G W Yates' shops stood on either side of Market Place, where the square narrowed and became Old Mill Gate. In the earlier photograph, taken around 1905, the Wellington Inn stands on the left, outside where two carts have come to rest.

This half timbered building was erected in 1552 in the area then known as The Shambles. It was used by the Byrom family as a drapery and was the birthplace of the writer, John Byrom, in 1692. By then a third storey had been added and it was turned into licensed premises in 1830. It was then called the Vintners Arms and, later, Kenyon Vaults. From 1865 it adopted the name by which we now know it, though its upper floors were used by mathematical instrument makers. By the end of the century, these rooms were taken over as Ye Olde Fyshing Tackle Shoppe. In the 1970s, the whole building was moved to what is now Shambles Square to make way for the Arndale Centre. There were any number of pubs and beerhouses in and around Market Place in the early 20th century. The Falstaff Hotel, pictured a few years after the First World War, near the entrance to Blue Boar Court, was where the founding delegate conference of the railway trade union ASLEF was held on 3 January, 1881.

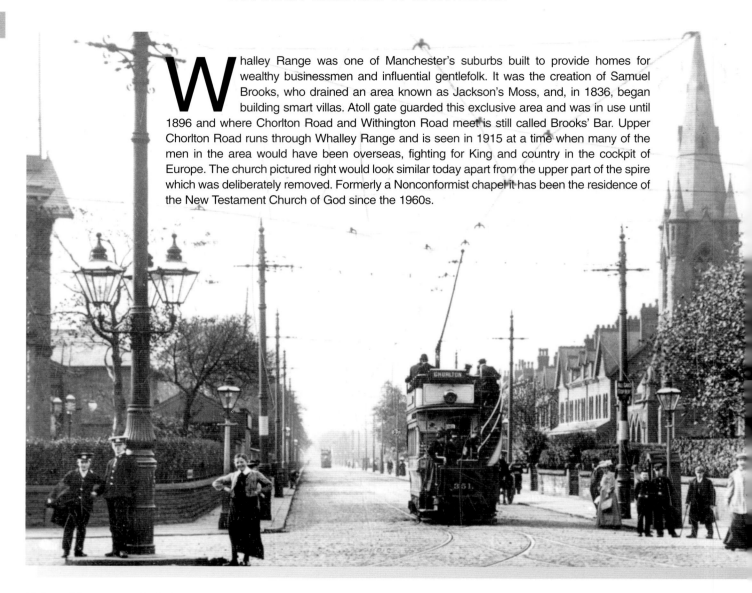

Whalley Range was one of Manchester's suburbs built to provide homes for wealthy businessmen and influential gentlefolk. It was the creation of Samuel Brooks, who drained an area known as Jackson's Moss, and, in 1836, began building smart villas. Atoll gate guarded this exclusive area and was in use until 1896 and where Chorlton Road and Withington Road meet is still called Brooks' Bar. Upper Chorlton Road runs through Whalley Range and is seen in 1915 at a time when many of the men in the area would have been overseas, fighting for King and country in the cockpit of Europe. The church pictured right would look similar today apart from the upper part of the spire which was deliberately removed. Formerly a Nonconformist chapel it has been the residence of the New Testament Church of God since the 1960s.

Below: A famous murder in the area occurred when it was at the height of its fashionable status, in the 1870s. PC Nicholas Cock, a Lancashire Constabulary beat officer, was killed only a short walk from along the road in the image above. Around midnight on 1 August, 1876, investigating a suspicious noise coming from the house of Samuel Gratrix, he was fatally shot, the bullet embedding itself in the boundary wall. The building, West Point, was later substantially extended on its eastern side to become the 'Seymour Hotel', but the place in the wall where the bullet lodged was marked, and visible on Woodside Road. The wall has since been demolished with the rest of the building. Two local farm labourers, the Habron brothers, were suspected and William Habron (aged 18) was tried and condemned for the murder, although there must have been some doubt, as the sentence was commuted. Some years later, an infamous criminal, Charles Peace, confessed to the murder before he was due for execution; because of this Habron was released.

As time goes on, the memories fade. Even so, this set of Market Street images might just bring to mind the occasional thought of what it was once like to head along one of the city's most popular retail areas. At the top of the road, coming out of Piccadilly, Lewis's department store dominated the corner. Founded in Liverpool in 1856 by David Lewis, our branch opened in 1877. It included a complete ballroom on one floor that was also in demand as an exhibition centre. It was Manchester's best known shop for over a century, but fell victim to a recession in trade and was bought by Owen Owen in 1991. It is now home to Primark. Modern Market Street is largely pedestrianised. The photograph from 1910 (above) is a reminder that petrol-engined cars and vans, electrically-powered trams and the simple horse and cart once worked in happy harmony on the cobbled highway. By the time that we reached the middle of the last century, animals and trams had disappeared from Market Street completely. The Arndale Centre, that mammoth complex of retail outlets, now dominates the northern side of the street. Built in the 1970s, it was redeveloped after the 1996 bombing by the IRA. It now occupies about 1.4 million square feet of retail space. It is not to everyone's taste and many long to see again the Victorian architecture that once abounded here.

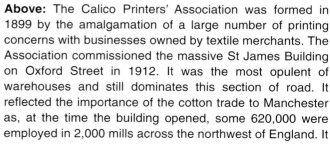

Above: The Calico Printers' Association was formed in 1899 by the amalgamation of a large number of printing concerns with businesses owned by textile merchants. The Association commissioned the massive St James Building on Oxford Street in 1912. It was the most opulent of warehouses and still dominates this section of road. It reflected the importance of the cotton trade to Manchester as, at the time the building opened, some 620,000 were employed in 2,000 mills across the northwest of England. It is in use today as offices and as a conference and exhibition centre. A variety of shops occupy the ground floor spaces. The Palace Theatre is located on the right in this inter-war photograph.

Above right: Even as late as 1924, goods were still being moved around by horse and cart. On Cannon Street, looking north towards High Street, modern lorries, some

Army war surplus, were transporting loads, but other traders still pinned their faith on their four legged friends. The period after the 1914-18 War was one in which those who had served their country either at home or abroad expected to be rewarded for their efforts. Prime Minister Lloyd George promised that the government would create a land fit for heroes. But it did not happen. The country was crippled by its war debt and hampered by a lack of investment in industry. Shipbuilding, the textile industry and coal mining experienced difficult times. We were heading for recession and the Depression of the late 1920s and 1930s.

Above: Seen from above, the Mount Street junction with Peter Street at the old YMCA corner in April 1938 was used for a massive advert for Player's Navy Cut cigarettes. This was a Nottingham business and one of the first to offer pre-packaged tobacco. Navy Cut, featuring a picture of a bearded sailor, was one of the earliest of the Player brands. The company was also a leader in introducing cigarette cards into its packets. One of the first sets, Castles and Abbeys, appeared in 1893. At the time that these vehicles crossed this junction, cards about footballers, aircraft and film stars were popular acquisitions. A mint set would set a collector back a small fortune today.

Top right: The woman pushing the toddler in the pram across the tramway on Alexandra Road, Moss Side, was chancing things a bit. Accidents with trams were not unusual. We do not know where she was off to in 1921, but it was unlikely to be the Edinburgh Hall on the opposite side of the road. This building contained a small dance hall on the first floor. The Park Cinema

that closed in 1939 was also in this block on the corner with Greame Street. Large residential parts of this area were subject to regeneration programmes from the mid-1970s onwards.

Below: King Street was a major centre of Lancashire's banking industry. Many fine buildings associated with finance remain and have been awarded listed status. During the inter-war years it continued to be influential and, as we can see, now incorporated a number of retail outlets. Today, much of the shopping area in this vicinity is regarded as belonging to the upmarket category. The area between Cross Street and Deansgate is largely pedestrianised.

Above: Looking from about Princess Street towards the direction of Market Street, the building on the right on the near corner with King Street was designed by Charles Heathcote. It is now occupied by Northern Rock. Nearly twenty years later, Heathcote built the baroque style Lloyds Bank. This handsome edifice, made of

Portland stone and with carvings by Earp, Hobbs and Miller, was erected on the site of the old Town Hall. On the other side of the road, at the corner of St Ann Street, is the building now used by the Alliance and Leicester. It was built by Heathcote and Rawle in 1901. The architecture from the 1930s shows little change today in this part of the city, for which we must be thankful.

Bottom left: The Town Hall, that wonderful piece of Gothic Victorian architecture, dominates Albert Square. Completed in 1877, it was the work of the prominent architect Alfred Waterhouse (1830-1905). He was also responsible for many other famous buildings, including London's Natural History Museum and the Royal Infirmary in Liverpool. The creation of the square arose from a project to honour the memory of Queen Victoria's husband, Prince Albert, who died in 1861. The central area contains a memorial to him, within which stands a marble figure of Albert created by Matthew Noble. There are several other statues within sight of the Town Hall, including one of William Gladstone who served as Prime Minister in the late 19th century on four separate occasions.

Below: Buses swept round the corner of Parker Street and Mosley Street in October 1957, showing how open this area still was. Even over a decade after the war had finished, there were still parts of the city that showed elements of bomb damage. Large warehouses had once stood on and around here, but they were destroyed in late 1940. Staines Inlaid Linoleum, J Templeton and Peel, Watson and Company were reduced to rubble as fires swept across here and Portland Street. Still, motorists were able to use some of these sites as parking places until they were redeveloped The advert for BEA above the cars suggested that Mancunians might just be thinking of flying across the Channel for their holidays instead of driving the Ford Popular over the Menai Bridge.

A fantastic view across the rooftops of central Manchester in 1969, the same year as Australian media baron Rupert Murdoch purchased the largest selling British Sunday newspaper, The News of the World. Very prominent in the background is the Co-operative Insurance Tower, or CIS Tower building on Miller Street. It was completed in 1962 and rises to 387 feet in height. The Grade II listed building, which houses Co-operative Financial Services, a part of The Co-operative Group, is Manchester's second-tallest building and the tallest office building outside London.

To the right of shot we can see the Royal Exchange, a grade II listed Victorian building. Much of the building that you see today, at the corner of Cross Street and Market Street, was built by Mills and Murgatroyd between 1869 and 1874 and modified by Bradshaw, Gass and Hope between 1914 and 1921. The building was seriously damaged during World War II when it took a direct hit from a bomb during a German air raid in the Manchester Blitz at Christmas in 1940. The interior was rebuilt with a smaller trading area. The top stages of the clock tower, which had been destroyed, were replaced in a simpler form. Trading ceased in 1968, and the building was threatened with demolition.

Pictured front, centre of the main photograph is the Old Wellington Inn public house. Grade II listed, it is the oldest surviving Tudor building of its kind in Manchester and it was built in 1552 next to the market square on what is now Market Street. In 1554 part of it became a draper's shop, owned by the Byrom family and the writer John Byrom was born there in 1692. The building had a third storey added to it in the 17th century. In 1830 the building became a licensed public house, known as the Vintners Arms, and later the Kenyon Vaults. By 1865 the ground floor of the building was known as the Wellington Inn. Later, in 1897, the upper floors were used as a fishing tackle shop, known as "Ye Olde Fyshing Tackle Shoppe" as can be seen above. In the

1970s the height of the building was raised by 1.4 metres, and the whole structure was relocated to make space for development of the Arndale Centre. The Old Wellington Inn is now part of Shambles Square, which was created in 1999, and is in close proximity to Manchester Cathedral.

Below: Parts of Parker Street are probably somewhere beneath the Piccadilly Plaza, later renamed City Tower, these days. It was built in the 1960s by Covell Matthews to the left of these bus shelters that were in the process of being erected on 26 August, 1958. This was around the time that our recovery from the austerity postwar years seemed to be almost complete. Seen from the Portland Street end of Piccadilly Gardens, though much remodelled this is still a main centre of public transport in the city. Both buses and trams, the latter back in fashion, can be caught from here.

Right: Brown Street is something of a backwater that runs across King Street. In 1975, its shops epitomised the architectural style of the late 60s and 70s. The style was rectangular and, to be honest, quite bland. Individuality was out and conformity in. The Market Centre had a link to Market Street and it was here that you could do some underground shopping. Entry was gained to this area via escalators that took you down into the bowels of the earth, or so it seemed. After the area was redeveloped, shoppers in the basement at Tesco tried to imagine that they were back among shops such as Oasis, Habeas Corpus and Goldmine.

Below: With university buildings and the small All Saints park close by, Grosvenor Square, on Oxford Road, was a busy spot in 1958. The bobby directing traffic was on the central island at the junction with Sidney Street. His job is now done by a Pelican crossing, an electrically controlled safety measure for pedestrians first seen in 1969. It replaced the similar, but less effective, Panda crossing that had been in operation since 1962. Obviously, this policeman was only on part-time traffic duties. Those with a longer stint in the middle of the highway tended to wear distinctive white over-arm pieces and gloves to match.

ENTERTAINMENT, LEISURE & PASTIMES

Belle Vue Zoological Gardens opened in 1836. They were initially intended as a place where genteel middle classes could come and enjoy the grounds and gardens, as well as the dancing arranged on open air platforms during balmy summer evenings. Before long, it became one of the most popular entertainment centres in the country, with a zoo, fairground rides, a roller coaster and a scenic railway. By 1900, Belle Vue had grown into a mighty complex that also included a covered dance hall, restaurants and an arena for firework displays. It became even more popular in the 20th century with the addition of the King's Hall that hosted a variety of events such as wrestling bouts, pop concerts, exhibitions and the like. A speedway team and rugby league side were based at Belle Vue and, at their peak, the various attractions brought in million visitors each year. The amusement park closed in 1980, three years after the zoo. The site was cleared in 1987. All that remains today is a greyhound racing stadium.

Below: Boggart Hole Clough is one of those places with a name that southerners think is drawn from fiction. Knotty Ash and Oswaldtwistle fall into the same bracket. But, as Mancunians know, it is real enough, the site of an ancient wooded valley and now a large municipal park. Legend has it that the valley, or 'clough', was once populated by mischievous sprites known locally as 'boggarts' who made their homes in holes in the ground. In 1935, just as they had done for many years before, families strolled around the pathways and gardens as they took the air on the edge of Blackley, a few miles away from the grime of the industrial city. The 190 acre site still offers relaxation for some and brisk recreation for others.

Right: Trams were one of the main forms of public transport and served our city particularly well either side of the Great War. This trio of vehicles were at one of the tram stations at the Piccadilly terminus. Across the road, Lyons Popular State Café provided refreshment for shoppers and office workers. This building, with its exotic Moorish styled turrets, had once been the site from where the White Bear Hotel dispensed both nourishment and accommodation, for business travellers in particular. It was largely remodelled in the early 1900s, becoming the Kardomah Café about 1910 before being taken into Lyons' chain. A branch of Superdrug can be found there today. The Piccadilly Cinema next door was built in 1922 by Percy Hothersall in a 'Beaux Arts' style. It replaced the former Mosley Hotel building and is here seen showing the 1933 Jessie Matthews' movie, 'The Good Companions'. After it closed as a cinema the building was used by Littlewoods and, more recently, Boots opened a section of retail space here.

Below: Palatine Road, the B5167, is one of the major arterial routes around the southeast of the city centre, linking Wilmslow Road with Princess Parkway. This Picture House that closed over half a century ago took its name from the road. Seen in 1924, it was charging a high price for admission as most places dealt in pennies, rather than the minimum of a shilling being charged here.

Above: Cosy gatherings and restful times, lounging in the rays of the summer sun or just frolicking in the gentle waters of the River Bollin: did we think that we would ever see the like again? There had been too many Augusts when we glanced anxiously at the skies or tuned into the radio to listen to news of some mighty battle being fought on a foreign field. But, now it was 1945 and this was our first summer of freedom for what seemed like an age. The river banks at Ashley, near Hale, made a perfect place to picnic in the shadow of Castle Hill. Was that a bluebird flying past on its way to the white cliffs of Dover?

Right: At the start of the war, the Government decreed that all major public gatherings were to be banned. Spectator sports, cinemas and the like would have been badly hit if the immediate public outcry had not been heeded. A quick rethink concluded that the upkeep of morale was more important than the risks run should Goering's Luftwaffe come to call. Manchester Racecourse continued to pull in large crowds of punters, as in this scene from 1941 when the wartime substitute St Leger was held here. Despite its name, the venue was actually at Castle Irwell in Salford. It had been sited in several places over the years since it began in the 17th century, but these were always within the Salford boundaries. It became a tradition that this course hosted the final racing of the flat season, the highlight being the November Handicap. The last race held here in 1963 was won by a horse ridden by Lester Piggott.

Left: At one time you could spend a different night, spread over several weeks, in every cinema in the city without visiting the same picture house twice. The Deansgate was just one of so many that had to start battling for its existence against the growing twin threats of bingo halls and television. In 1959, it hoped that 'The Return of the Fly' and 'The Alligator People', a pair of rather silly 'X' rated so-called horror movies, would pack them in. However, it had some success when it was rebranded as the ABC Deansgate, but it never regained the same level of popularity it once had. Situated at 68-74 Deansgate, its façade is much the same today in its current guise as The Moon Under Water, a Wetherspoon's bar.

How things change, but in the end are just the same. A McDonald's fast food outlet now stands at 36 Oxford Street where once Lyons restaurant chain had an outlet. This company, founded by Joseph Lyons in 1887, also made its own range of bread, cakes, pies, tea, coffee and ice cream that it provided in its tea shops and corner houses. The white and gold fronted teashops occupied prominent positions in many high streets and in the process became a household name. Next door is one of the city's first purpose-built cinemas. The Oxford Picture House opened on 15 December, 1911, with a film of "Captain Scott's Expedition to the South Pole" and was to be the first of a number of cinema's along Oxford Street. Even today, the name 'The Picture House' can be seen in the stonework above the entrance. Later to be re-named 'New Oxford Theatre' it was equipped to screen CinemaScope films in 1953, and became the home of 20th Century Fox films in central Manchester. One such film, 'The High and the Mighty' from 1954, starring John Wayne is a fine example of this new development in cinema projection. Some years later, in 1959, its seats were full again, as the very popular Audrey Hepburn starred in 'The Nun's Story', a Warner Brothers movie set in the Second World War. Now known as the 'New Oxford Picture House', it was taken over by the Rank Organisation and was their roadshow house, playing long runs of "Ben Hur" and other blockbusters. In later years after this type of film dried up, and the 'New Oxford' began playing less popular films. It was closed on 25 October, 1980, with David Carradine in "The Long Riders".

Below: The Odeon Cinema was one of a number of cinemas and theatres on Oxford Street. The Odeon was originally opened in 1930 as the Paramount Theatre and was built as a showpiece for the Paramount Film Company

in America, to the designs of F. Verity and S. Beverley, who also built the Plaza Theatre in Lower Regent Street, London. This picture was taken not long after the opening and at the time, the Theatre had seating for 2,920 people on two levels, Stalls and Balcony, a fully equipped stage and fly tower, dressing rooms, and orchestra pit and its very own Wurlitzer 4 manual 20 rank publix No.1 Theatre Organ.The Paramount was used primarily for film but also put on live shows on its large stage and was built to be operating in the then popular cine-variety era. Showing on screen at the time was 'The Beloved Bachelor', starring Paul Lukas and Dorothy Jordan, or maybe you would have preferred to watch Joan Barry in Ebb Tide? In 1973 the Theatre was sub divided and became

a Twin Screen Cinema and the original Wurlitzer organ was removed and reinstalled in the Free Trade Hall, just a hundred yards from its original home. Despite the addition of further screens over a number of years, the building was closed in September 2004.

Below: This is a face on view of the The Plaza from 1940, many readers may recognise this as Tiffany's nightclub as it became known. After the war The Plaza and The Ritz were very popular places to go after having a drink in Tommy Ducks. There seemed to be something for everyone advertised in this photograph. The luxurious ballroom had to cater for parties, dancing, weddings and even carnival and surprises. There was even a billiard room downstairs for the guys. It would certainly be a surprise to some readers to hear that city worker in the 50s & 60s used to nip into the Plaza to have a jive at lunchtime. They could have a snack lunch and a soft drink whilst enjoying the music of DJ Jimmy Savile, in his pre 'Top Of The Pops' days. Others may remember DJ 'Mad Mike' who shared the disco duties with a young 'Hairy Cornflake', Dave Lee Travis. It certainly appears like the place to be in those days, whether day or night and will probably have many happy memories for our readers.

The building on the corner of Portland Street, where Schweppes tonic was advertised in 1964, has now been replaced by a Premier Travel Inn and the Circus Casino. Further along Oxford Street, Bovril is no longer available and the site is mainly an office block with some ground floor retail space. In between, the Odeon Cinema is also no more. It closed in 2004, despite having undergone extensive renovations in the 1970s and again in the 1990s. It opened originally as the Paramount in 1930, with a capacity for nearly 3,000 patrons.

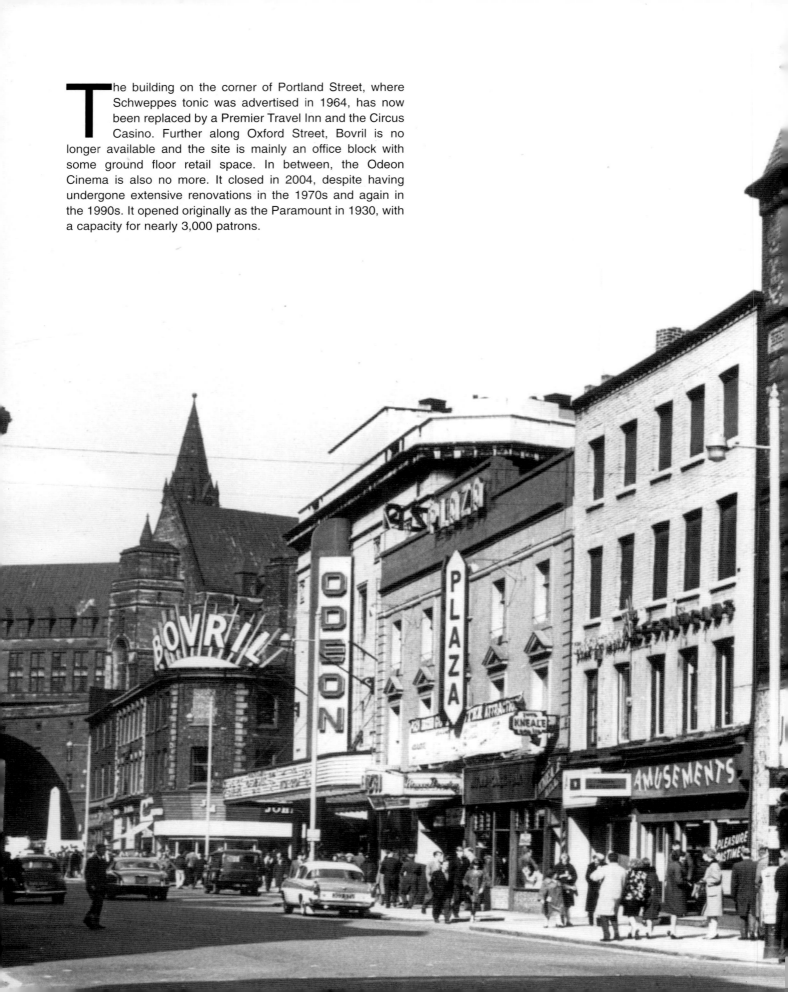

Above: The date given for this photograph is 1957, though the costumes worn by people in the crowd at Belle Vue fun fair would appear to be from a decade earlier. The Caterpillar remained a popular ride for many years and was a rather more thrilling experience than the Ocean Wave which was one of Belle Vue's first amusements, and was popular during the 1920s. Tame by today's hair raising standards, the Ocean Wave was built after the 'Sea on Land' type of ride that was common in Victorian times. The bridge of a ship was created on a large roundabout amid scenery that was painted to look like storm dashed waves. As an internal machine rotated the roundabout, small boats set among the waves rose and fell to the accompaniment of squeals of delight from the boats' occupants. Other amusements that were popular during the very early years of Belle Vue was its fledgling zoo. Back then people had little experience of the wider world and its fauna, and six policemen had to control the huge crowds who mobbed the amusement park to see an orangutan billed as the 'Wild Man of Borneo'.

Right: The Scala was the third cinema to open in Britain when it opened its door for the first time in 1912. Also known as Cine City it was located on Wimslow Road, Withington, next to the splendid White Lion public house, which was built in the mid-19th century. Before the advent of "talkies", the Scala had a resident female cinema pianist. During the 1930s the popularity of the new 'picture houses' grew rapidly, with 109 in Manchester at its peak. Many people visited The Scala three or four times a week. Regularly seen at the cinema in the 1920s was local lad, Robert Donat, who went on to become an Oscar winning actor. After the war, the popularity of cinemas waned as more people acquired televisions, and by 1965 there were only 40 cinemas left in Manchester. Seen here in this 1967 photograph are posters for three popular films of the time, which have as their stars such household names as, James Mason, Michael Crawford and Eric Sykes. Increased competition sadly resulted in the closure of the cinema in 2001.

Right: During the 1950s, young people aped their American cousins in their choice of music, hair styles and dress sense. Young women adopted a more casual look, favouring jeans, hipsters, bobby sox and sweaters that were either tight fitting or sloppy Joes. Denim became popular with young people as a statement of rebellion and independence. Instead of turning to the glamorous world of the movies and high society, teens began to take their cues from the lower classes. The vanity cases contained all a girl needed for a quick touching up of the features. Their appearance contrasted dramatically with the demure look of the more mature women alongside them at Central Station in 1958. Although photographed together, they are worlds and generations apart.

WARTIME

Above: In the months leading up to the outbreak of war in 1939, the population became increasingly worried about the prospect of gas being used as a weapon against us. The mood was not helped when Liddell Hart, a government adviser, warned that we could expect 250,000 deaths in the first week of hostilities. Some 38 million gas masks were issued by the end of the summer and everyone, especially schoolchildren, was trained in their use. Kiddies carried their masks in little cardboard boxes to and from school and drills were conducted to help them get used to wearing the strange looking contraptions that might just save their lives.

Top right: With petrol and diesel in short supply during the war, Manchester Corporation turned to other sources to help fuel its public transport. This bus, pictured on 26 January 1940, was one of an experimental type that had been adapted to access gas contained in the bag on its roof. Other local authorities experimented with gas contained in a trailer dragged behind their vehicles. Safety was an ongoing issue with

these contraptions, as was the range a bus could manage on one bagful. Although not rare, such buses were not widely used as there were also difficulties faced in successfully converting the engines to accept the gas flow.

Right: Although America did not help us out officially in the last war until it was forced to after the attack on Pearl Harbour, it had been supplying aid in one form or another by providing goods and equipment where it could. The lorry in the background owed its existence to this backdoor friendship. The Food Flying Squad was a service created by Lady Reading. She was the founder of the Women's Voluntary Service and her members staffed this unit that ran mobile canteens that supported the work of firemen, the police and heavy rescue personnel during and after an air raid. Locals, such as these seen in 1941, also took advantage of the refreshments as they attempted to come to terms with the terrible damage done to their homes and neighbourhood.

Above: These members of the Air Raid Precautions (ARP) service had not come for a cuppa at the Kardomah. They were taking part in an important exercise. Sporting the gasmasks that made them look like something out of an episode of Dr Who, these men had an important role in 1941. They were part of a decontamination unit that was trained to deal with the aftermath of an air raid. Initially, their role was expected to be one of attending to problems created by poison or gas bombs. When this threat did not materialise, their expertise was brought to bear on chemical and gas leaks in homes and industrial premises, so the lessons learned during ARP training came in very useful anyway.

Left: We had seen what mustard gas and its companions could do to soldiers in the trenches during the previous war and now the Germans had powerful bombers that could release large canisters of noxious stuff from the skies. In the end, no such attacks were made as the enemy feared that we could more than match such assaults. But, in the beginning, we took no chances. In the months preceding the outbreak of war, every child was issued with a gas mask and taught how to use it. Additionally, civil defence units mounted instructional sessions that offered practical advice for action during and after an air raid. Here, people manning a mobile first aid post gave practical advice in this training exercise.

Above: Great concern was shown for our children at the start of World War II. The nation felt a combined sense of parenthood. To this end, under Operation Pied Piper, thousands of kiddies were whisked away from their homes and out to homes in safer and, usually, more rural areas. These children, with their names on luggage labels tied to their lapels, wished tearful goodbyes to their parents as a series of trains took them to their destinations on 2 September, 1939. The following day, Prime Minister Chamberlain announced on the radio that war had been declared. The young evacuees listened to the broadcast in strange surroundings. Some enjoyed the adventure, but most were homesick and longed to see their parents again. The majority did so within a few months.

The week beginning 23 February, 1942, was designated Warship Week in Manchester and was repeated in other towns and cities across the country at various times during the 1939-45 War. This was one of several National Savings drives held that promoted the idea of a community adopting a Royal Navy vessel. A savings target would be set, dependent upon the size of the local population, and progress towards the figure was often marked by a thermometer mounted on the side of a large building. Cities usually aimed to provide a battleship or aircraft carrier, while towns and villages focused on cruisers and destroyers. Practical assistance was also given with schools, churches and local groups providing gloves, socks and balaclavas for the ships' crews. Officers and

crewmen from adopted ships visited to offer thanks and mounted parades in the streets past cheering crowds. The HMS Nelson, for which Mancunians were collecting, was not a new battleship, but one that was costing a considerable amount in repairs. It had been badly damaged in September 1941 by a torpedo dropped from an Italian plane and it took help from our city's cash to effect repairs that got her back into service by May 1942. This group of photographs shows that the RAF also contributed to the military displays with models of its fighter planes and barrage balloon defence of our skies. The little lad in Army uniform was one of the reasons for which our country mounted the sternest of opposition to the fascists who attempted to dominate Europe.

Right: During the war life changed for everybody, including children for whom the war years were a time of anxiety. Children had to grow up quickly during wartime, as many had to look after themselves and younger siblings while their mothers worked. Seen here are two small boys in gas masks being guided by a warden. The photograph was taken near to St Joseph's police station in Longsight, Manchester. The boys look quite relaxed as they receive instruction, as every effort was made to accustom children to the frightening and claustrphobic gas masks that made the wearers look like fearsome monsters. The masks, when new, were very stiff and tight and uncomfortable to wear. Some may have found these drills hard to take seriously, especially older children, when they discovered blowing air out through the rubber made 'rude' noises.

Left: No one liked wearing the gas masks, but young mothers with babies had a particularly difficult time during the Second World War, when masks were issued to all British civilians. There was a very real fear in Britain that German bombers would drop poison gas bombs. Babies, however, had special cradle-like respirators which would only be issued out if an emergency situation arose. Babies were put inside the case and when all the covering flaps were folded and the straps closed up. The baby was totally enclosed, fresh air was pumped in, using a hand pump, through a filter on the side ensuring the baby inhaled no gas. Mothers were greatly affected by the thought of their babies suffocating inside their gas masks. The government thought that younger children would be scared of the gas masks so they produced a specially designed version which became known as a 'Mickey Mouse' gas mask, which was brightly coloured in red and blue.

This page: It was possibly the acute wartime shortages of food and supplies which made doctors, health workers and mothers alike very aware of the health of the new generation, and children were carefully weighed, measured and immunised against illness, as can be seen in this Child Welfare Clinic picture from Manchester, in 1950. It is worth remembering only two years earlier, health secretary Aneurin Bevan had opened Park Hospital in Manchester and this marked the birth of the NHS system and the climax of a hugely ambitious plan to bring good healthcare to all. For many of us, it is difficult to imagine life before the NHS,

when healthcare was unreliable and treatment had to be paid for. During the war, children had their own ration books which entitled pre-school children to an allowance of cod-liver oil and orange juice. Long before the advent of the cod liver oil capsule, the recommended spoonful of cod liver oil was administered to the youngest children every day. Children might have screwed up their noses at the fishy taste, but the nourishing cod liver oil went a long way towards keeping them healthy. The vitamin-packed orange juice was far more palatable, and artful mothers would often use the orange juice as a bribe. Later it became available as 'cod liver oil and malt', a totally acceptable brown sticky substance that tasted like toffee and had to be spooned out of a large jar. It has been said that child nutrition in the 1950s was superior to today, according to researchers - despite the food shortages of the post war period. Modern children fare worse for intake of several key nutrients, including fibre, calcium, vitamins and iron. In fact, rather surprisingly, the 1950s diet was almost in line with current recommendations on healthy eating for children.

Left: A series of morale and fundraising exercises were held during the last war. There were Warship Weeks, Spitfire Weeks, Tank Banks, Wings for Victory, War Bond drives and many more. There was a constant urging to collect salvage, make do and mend and to dig for victory. In May 1944, it was the turn of a week set aside to Salute the Soldier. Army personnel marched through Piccadilly and we were all encouraged to head off to the post office or bank and make our contribution by purchasing more Savings Certificates.

Below: A scene of joy and happiness as servicemen join in with members of the public in Manchester to celebrate VJ Day. The surrender of Japan on 15 August, 1945, finally ending the conflict that had torn families apart for six years. Celebrations were taking place the length and bredth of the country and Manchester was no exception, with singing, dancing and drinking, that was to last for two days. The joy was mirrored across the city as Mancunians let their hair down. The central areas began to fill up with revellers from midnight on 14 August, long before the Lord Mayor made the official announcement from the Town Hall at 10am the next day. Vast crowds congregated in Piccadilly, singing and dancing along to the public address system which was broadcasting the popular tunes of the day. In St Peter's Square, George Formby was entertaining the crowds in his own inimitable way. Amidst the celebrations there were also services of thanksgiving in churches, as people for the first time began to reflect on what had happened to loved ones and friends lost in the conflict. Many Mancunian wives and mothers had not heard from their menfolk literally for years, and had no idea whether they would ever see them again. Whatever your circumstances on that day there was a wave of Patriotism, relief and sheer exuberance that only people attending fully appreciated.

EVENTS & OCCASIONS

Below right: We knew them as Red Indians long before they became Native Americans. Taking their place on the tram at Belle Vue in 1903 were braves, squaws, papooses and a few chiefs. But, the pride of place went to William Cody (1846-1917). Better known as Buffalo Bill, he was a true son of the Wild West. He was a former US Army scout and supplier of meat to railway workers in Kansas, hence the nickname. He won a gallantry medal during his army service and his exploits were recorded and exaggerated by the writer, Ned Buntline. Cody cashed in on his reputation by establishing an original touring show that developed into an international success. Bareback riding, sharpshooting, rope tricks, cattle branding, mock skirmishes with covered wagons under attack and stagecoaches being robbed packed in audiences wherever Buffalo Bill went. He toured Europe on eight occasions, performing before crowned heads and the general populace alike.

Left: Two provincial cities were selected each year to receive a royal visit from King Edward VII and Queen Alexandra. In July 1905, it was the turn of Sheffield and Manchester to be honoured. The royal couple were guests at Knowsley Hall, the ancestral home of the Earls of Derby, and it was from there that they travelled into our city. The day was declared a Bank Holiday in Manchester, Salford and Stretford and this enabled thousands more than might normally have taken to the streets to enjoy the occasion. The royal open topped carriage passes through Piccadilly and people lined the pavements, hung out of windows and stood precariously on roof tops to get a glimpse.

Below: Claude Grahame-White (1879-1959) was a pioneer in the early years of powered flight. He gained particular fame as the first pilot to make a night flight, doing so in 1910 during the London to Manchester air race sponsored by the Daily Mail. He became well known for a variety of daring manoeuvres, including landing his Farman biplane on Executive Avenue, close to the White House in Washington. Here he can be seen after an aerial display at Fallowfield Sports Ground on 13 July, 1912. By then, he had established a flying school at Hendon and soon developed an interest in the military potential of aircraft, experimenting with fitting weapons and bombs to his flying machines.

Right: The Bradford district lies a couple of miles northeast of the city centre. It was an economically deprived area, but the residents of Beaumont Street had a pride in being British. On 22 June, 1911, George V was crowned as our monarch. Out came the bunting and up went the flags. These folk may have been poor, but you were not going to stop them having a knees up. After all, life was tough for the

working classes, so this was a good excuse to blow off a bit of steam. There was a proper community spirit around here as everybody helped one another. Children called neighbouring adults 'aunt' and 'uncle'. There was true sense of a common purpose.

Bottom right: It is hard to imagine what these children in Lancashire would have made of this elderly Indian man, dressed in a loin cloth and wearing sandals. Crowds throng to catch a glimpse of Hindu leader, Mohandas Karamchand Gandhi (Mahatma), who had accepted the invitation issued by Mr Corder Catchpool, of Greenfield Mill, to visit Lancashire and see for himself the effects India's boycott on cotton goods had had on the workers there. In September 1931, the statesman met groups of unemployed cotton workers from the Lancashire textile industry. In round table talks with the British Government, Gandhi pleaded for an honourable and equal partnership between Britain and India, held not by force but "by the silken cord of love". He found the odds very much against him, however, as he pointed

out the poverty in his homeland. Gandhi was born on October 2, 1869, in Porbandar, India. It is said he spoke English with an Irish accent, for one of his first teachers was an Irishman. He studied law in London between 1888 and 1891 and set sail to South Africa in 1893 where he opened his own law office. In 1915, Gandhi returned to India permanently. He brought a reputation as a leading Indian nationalist, theorist and organiser. It is ironic that he was assassinated on 30 January, 1948, the year after India became independent from British rule.

Left: It was a great day for Mancunians when King George V was driven into the city. Here his procession, with the monarch and his consort, Queen Mary, passed Piccadilly on 14 July 1913. Thousands lined the streets, shouting 'Hurrah' and throwing their hats into the air. Union flags swung patriotically and everybody expressed a pride in being British. It was a time when we still had a mighty empire, but there was change in the air. There was unrest in the Balkans that would come to a head a year later when Archduke Franz Ferdinand was assassinated, throwing Europe into a bitter conflict.

Below: King George V and Queen Mary visited in October 1921 and, as part of their duties, presided at a ceremony to mark the completion of remodelling work on the Royal Exchange building. This couple was the first of the House of Windsor to rule our land. George, as the grandson of Victoria and Albert, was actually a member of the Saxe-Coburg-Gotha family, but adopted the Windsor name in 1917. Not surprisingly, considering that we were at war with Germany, it was felt that the change was entirely appropriate. Although born in London, Queen Mary was also of Germanic stock, her father having been the Duke of Teck.

Left: The sun was shining on 8 June, 1939, and the nursing staff at the Duchess of York Hospital for Babies in Burnage, took advantage of the good weather to get some sun for their infant charges. Elsewhere, the storm clouds of war were gathering and it would not be long before these ladies of the lamp practised fitting specially designed gas masks onto the tiny tots. Formerly known as the Manchester Babies' Hospital, it was founded in 1914 in Levenshulme, moving to Cringle Hall, Burnage in 1919. Within 10 years, the number of patients had risen from double figures to 430. A new wing was opened by the Duchess of York in 1935 and the hospital's name was changed at the same time. It closed in 1986.

Above: We had three kings in 1936, just as we had done in 1066. George V died in January and his eldest son became King Edward VIII. However, he was never crowned and had abdicated before the end of the year. He was succeeded by his brother as George VI and the latter enjoyed his Coronation Day on 12 May, 1937, the same date originally reserved for his brother. The general public decided that it would push the boat out as it had not had a decent street party since Armistice Day, nearly 20 years earlier. Tenth, Street in the heart of Trafford Park, is now part of the industrial complex where such companies as Lamba Trading are based, but it was once part of a thriving community of terraced housing. Like everywhere else, the residents said, 'Long live the king'.

Left: Some of us can well remember Market Street as it was before the Arndale Centre came to change the face of this part of the city. In 1962, preparations were afoot to decorate the street ready for Christmas. Hepworths, on the right, was a top name in tailoring at this time. It would later rebrand itself as Next. Further along, Timpsons continues to have success, but John Collier is no longer 'the window to watch'. It was taken over by Burton in 1985 and the brand name discontinued.

On 23 May, 1952, the Runbaken Electrical Products Company premises at 71 Oxford Road were gutted by a major fire. The company marketed electrical test equipment and also had a history of providing coils, magnetos and other electrical goods. In 1919, the Runbaten Magneto Company, as it was once known, also produced a type of motorcycle that was a prototype of the scooter favoured by mods in the 1960s. However, this one was rather primitive. It had a 0.5 horsepower electric motor powered from a large 6 volt battery mounted on the foot platform. It could only average 9 mph and had a range of 12 miles before a recharge was needed. Not surprisingly, the idea was soon abandoned! More successfully, Runbaken supplied parts to the aircraft industry.

The 1973 Manchester Festival was one of the best ever held. There were any number of floats to see, organised by community groups, churches, theatres, industrial firms, breweries, car companies and the rest. The Grenadier Guards even took the opportunity to set up a recruiting post in the hope of attracting a bit of custom. All along the streets, locals took up vantage points from where they could get a good view of the gaily decorated parade that passed before them. Children loved the Manchester Evening News float with its cartoon dog peeking over the cab of the lorry and there were also attractive contributions from the shire horses pulling the Tetley dray, the humorous dust particles on the Hoover float and the pretty girls in miniskirts promoting British Airways. There was fun in the air and that was no better expressed than in a special competition for the best smile of the day.

The festival queen got a special cheer as she was driven along, sitting on the back of an open topped limousine. Scouts, cubs, brownies and guides walked behind their flags and marching bands went past, amid much baton twirling, and everyone agreed that a jolly good time was had by all. The festival has now turned into the Manchester Day Parade and latterly attracted a magnificent 70,000 onto the streets in celebration. There are a number of special events in the city, such as the parades tied to the Caribbean Carnival, Irish Festival and Manchester Pride, but none of these are as all-inclusive as the Manchester Day Parade.

Above: Some thought that celebrations to mark royal anniversaries had become old hat by 1977. Gloom mongers predicted that the Queen's Silver Jubilee would be a damp squib. How wrong they were and how glad we were that their predictions were just as miserable as those making them. The nation toasted 'good old Liz' and partied on the streets just like it had a generation earlier when she was crowned our monarch in Westminster Abbey. Residents on Cranswick Street, in Moss Side, were just like everyone else. They raised their glasses to Her Majesty and said, 'Cheers'.

Top right: Prince Philip, Duke of Edinburgh landed at Platt Fields in a Royal Navy helicopter. He had already learned to fly, having qualified as a pilot with the RAF in 1953. Three years later, he got his helicopter wings and achieved a private pilot's licence in 1959, the year of this visit to Fallowfield. The land here was owned from medieval times by the Platt family until being sold to Ralph Worsley, a textile merchant, in 1625. The grand manor house was built in 1764 and is now home to Manchester Costume Museum. The estate was bought by the Corporation from the Worsley family in 1907. Whilst in Manchester, Prince Philip officiated at the opening of two new halls of residence for the University.

Right: Looking very dapper as he shared a joke with dignitaries on his way out of the Town Hall, Prince Charles was just 25 back in 1974. At this time he was heavily involved in establishing his military career, following in the tradition of several previous Princes of Wales. He served on a destroyer and several frigates, as well as qualifying as a helicopter pilot. He was the heir to the crown and, of course, still is nearly four decades later. He would be a long time in the regal shadow of Queen Elizabeth because she is only the second British monarch to exceed 60 years on the throne.

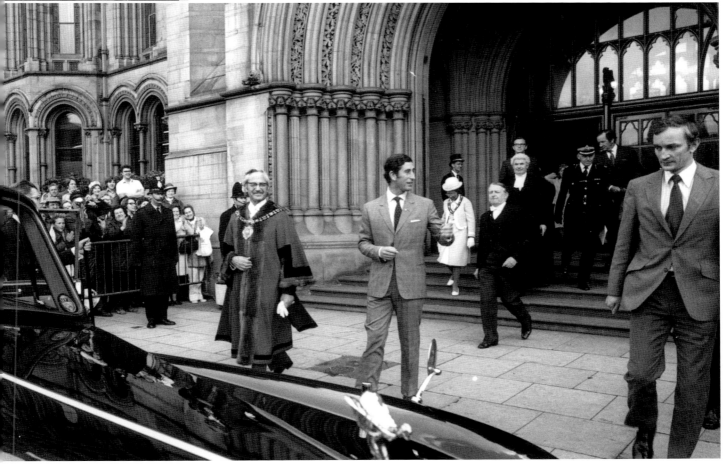

BUILDINGS & MONUMENTS

Above: The Infirmary relocated to this new building on Oxford Road, opposite the Whitworth Art Gallery, in 1908. King Edward VII performed the opening ceremony. The King was especially grateful to the medical profession as it had helped save his life when carrying out a difficult operation for the appendicitis that laid him low in 1902, delaying his coronation for a while. Manchester Infirmary suffered fire and bomb damage during World War II, but was restored to much of its former glory during peacetime. The hospital has been much enlarged in the last 25 years. In the summer of 2009 came the latest additions, a new children's hospital and a new eye hospital. The modern site also includes St Mary's Hospital, specialising in maternity issues and baby care. The modern Infirmary is also a centre for research into a broad range of medical problems.

Right: Just the portals of the old White City exterior remain in place on Chester Road, not far from Manchester United's football ground. They sit outside a small retail park where once Gordon Pirie and his fellow athletes raced on a cinder track in the 1950s. Later, stock car racing was introduced, but the stadium was closed in 1982. White City was built on the site of the gardens founded in 1827 by the Botanical and Historical Society. The grounds had a large complex of buildings that included an impressive conservatory. By the early 20th century, interest had begun to wane and in 1907, when this photograph was taken, the White City Amusement Park was opened. Admission to the site was a humble sixpence (2.5p). A stadium was built on part of the site in 1927 and this section was used to house a speedway circuit and was also home to greyhound racing from 1930 onwards.

Left: The Victoria University of Manchester, to give it its full name, was founded in 1880, following on from its earlier guise as Owen's College and reflecting its place in the short-lived federal Victoria University that included colleges in Liverpool and Leeds. Manchester's university was eventually established as a separate entity of learning in its own right in July 1903. No fewer than 25 Nobel Prize winners have links with this university. They include the world-famous scientists Ernest Rutherford and Niels Bohr.

Left: The Midland Hotel is one of the city's most prestigious buildings. Standing across from St Peter's Square, on the corner with Lower Mosley Street, it was built to provide first class accommodation for passengers using Central Station, across the other side of Windmill Street. The Midland Railway Company arranged for its building as a counterbalance to the handsome St Pancras Hotel at the London end of the line. Designed by Charles Trubshaw, work began on the Midland Hotel in 1893, with a covered walkway linking it to Central Station, and partially completed by 1898. It was not, though, fully functional until 1903. In its heyday the hotel had a palm court, an elaborate concert hall, a winter garden, Russian and Turkish baths and a roof garden. Some 23 lifts carried guests to the floors where 400 bedrooms were dispersed along over three miles of corridors. A plaque on the hotel's façade marks the occasion on 4 May, 1904, when Charles Rolls and Henry Royce held a meeting that led to the formation of the Rolls Royce company. The Midland was regularly used by American cotton traders and one of the restaurants was named The Colony in their memory. It is rumoured that Adolf Hitler coveted the premises, earmarking it as a possible Nazi HQ if his invasion plans came to fruition. In 1959, Queen Elizabeth II and the Queen Mother dined here, the first time a serving British monarch had ever eaten in a public restaurant. The Beatles pop group was once refused entry to the French Restaurant as its members were 'inappropriately dressed'. This was the Midland, after all!

Above: In 1905, Central Station was celebrating its silver jubilee. It was built by the Cheshire Lines Committee and opened on 1 July, 1880. The handsome roof is 550 feet in length, with a span of 210 feet, rising to 90 feet high at is apex. The station was used by Midland Railway as a terminus to London's St Pancras. The station closed in 1969, about the same time as Exchange Station on the other side of the city centre. It fell into disrepair and the site became a car park, but was rescued in the mid 1980s and relaunched in 1986 as an exhibition centre generally referred to as G-Mex.

Above: The view of St Peter's Square dates from the mid-20th century. The light coloured establishment on the left was built for the Friends Provident Insurance Company that was founded by the Quakers, Tuke and Rowntree, in Bradford in 1832. It acquired Century Insurance in 1918 and added its name to its own. Now called simply Century House, this building is still in place on the corner with Dickinson Street. However, its companion behind the Cenotaph has gone, replaced some time ago by a block of retail, office and apartment units.

Below: The extension to the Town Hall, seen on the right, was built in the late 1930s to provide additional accommodation for local government services. It was linked to its parent building by two covered bridges over Lloyd Street. The handsome circular Central Library was erected on the edge of St Peter's Square, at the corner with Peter Street and Oxford Street, a few years earlier. Designed by E Vincent Harris, its rotunda style was influenced by the Pantheon in Rome. The library was officially opened on 17 July, 1934, by King George V. Edwin Lutyens' Cenotaph had been unveiled here some 10 years earlier.

Below: A solitary car waits at the traffic lights at the junction of Market Street, Corporation Street and Cross Street, and the block of shops and offices opposite wears a tired and desolate air. The signs above the shops tell us the reason, and forty years on the wording of the notices still conveys the anger and resentment of the traders in the area that was earmarked for redevelopment. 'Forced out after 50 years' the pawnbroker Prosser & Son's sign tells us bitterly, while Beaty Brothers on the corner spells it out for us: 'Premises to be Demolished'. The desperate protests had no effect however on those who had already decreed otherwise, and within months these old buildings that had served the city well had vanished for ever. Before long the thirty acre site would lose its pubs, shops, banks, hotels and shops and would bristle with tower cranes and scaffolding. A landscaped pedestrian area eventually emerged from the organised chaos to be appreciated by the next generation of shoppers who had never known Market Street as it was in this photograph. Just off picture to the right is the Royal Exchange, which was the centre of Manchester's commercial life for many years.

Above: Our city had been a Roundhead stronghold in the Civil War and, in memory of this, this statue to Oliver Cromwell was controversially erected by Liberal politicians in 1875. It is said that Queen Victoria, when asked a few years later to perform the opening ceremony at Manchester Town Hall, declined the invitation with the words, 'not while that infernal statue stands'. Standing close to the old Exchange Station, that closed in 1969, 'Old Ironsides' was known as 'the pedestrians' pal' because he slowed down passing traffic, but he was eventually moved on his way. After over a century in situ he was taken to Wythenshawe Hall as he, along with much else around him, was swept away in a phase of inner city development.

Below: This was the view along Victoria Street half a century ago before this part of the city was subjected to the major redevelopment that changed the scene forever. However, it

was not developers but the IRA that, in 1996, blew away the old Marks & Spencer building on the right. The Royal Exchange in the centre has survived damage wreaked by both Luftwaffe and terrorist bombs. This commodities exchange, the third on this site, became the largest trading room in England when it was extended in the 1920s. Trading ceased in 1968 and the building lay empty until the mid-1970s when it became a theatre.

Below: The prominent feature in this 1966 aerial picture is the radial design of Manchester prison on Southall Street. Construction of the Grade II listed building, formerly known as Strangeways, was completed in 1869 to replace the New Bailey Prison, in Salford, which closed in 1868. The prison designed by Alfred Waterhouse in 1862, with input from Joshua Jebb, cost £170,000, and had a capacity of 1,000 inmates. Its 234 ft high, mineret-like ventilation tower can be seen in the bottom

right of this aerial photograph. It has become a local landmark and a prominent feature of the north Manchester skyline. Originally, the prison contained an execution shed in B wing; however, after World War I a special execution room and cell for the condemned criminal was built. Strangeways was also one of the few prisons to have permanent gallows. The first execution was of twenty-year-old murderer Michael Johnson, hanged by William Calcraft on 29 March, 1869. The prison was open to both male and female prisoners until 1963 when the facility became male-only, and in 1980 it began to accept remand prisoners. In April of 1990 a riot broke out at Strangeways, when a total of 47 prisoners and 147 members of staff were injured, one prisoner died and some of the buildings were virtually destroyed.The prison was rebuilt and modernised in 1994 and is now known as Her Majesty's Prison, Manchester. The road running from top to bottom of the image is the A56.

The Cathedral is instantly recognisable in this trio of photographs dating from Edwardian times to the 1950s. Stand in the same place as the photographers today and things would not appear to have altered a great deal. The public conveniences have disappeared, as has the Old Curiosity Shop from the older image, but the latter's replacement on the corner with Cateaton Street is still there. Amidst whatever changes were taking place on either side, across the road and further along Victoria Street, the Cathedral was steadfast. It is sometimes known as St Mary's, though it also carries the names of two other saints, Denys and George. Its main body derives from the time when James Stanley was the Warden in the late 15th century, though a church dedicated to St Mary was mentioned 400 years earlier in the Domesday Book. The diocese of Manchester was created in 1847 and the newly designated cathedral greatly restored over several subsequent decades. The Cathedral also had to endure major repairs after the Christmas blitz on the city in 1940. Every single piece of stained glass was blown to smithereens and the chantry chapel and medieval Lady's Chapel were completely wrecked. It took nearly 20 years to repair what the enemy had done in a matter of minutes.

CHILDREN'S PLAYTIME

Right The influence of Errol Flynn in the 1940s is obvious here in a game involving bows and arrows. His playing of Robin Hood against Olivia de Havilland as Maid Marian had a ground-breaking impact for some little boys that remained with them to their teenage years (and in some cases even longer!). Cinema has always had an influence on children's re-enactment and performance of stories and fables. Certainly children in the 1940s rarely complained about boredom or having nothing to do. They simply grasped the nettle and worked out what they could turn it into and did it together.

Below: In 1948, children used their imagination to create play situations. They had heard from their older siblings about seeking out salvage during the war, so they put that experience to good use in peacetime. They foraged for stuff discarded from local shops on Rochdale Road. The cardboard boxes and containers could be used as soldiers' hats or stuck together to create a boat. In fact, they could be anything they wanted them to be. The boys on the left carried a box that once held iconic Jubbly ices. They were frozen orange juice blocks wrapped in cardboard containers. Lovely jubbly!

Above: Road safety was a major issue in Britain either side of the last war. In the 1930s, we had one of the worst records for accidents and casualties of any country in Europe. Although measures aimed at adults, such as driving tests, traffic lights and Belisha crossings, were introduced, it was not until the 1950s that proper consideration was given to educating our children. Then we had a wave of schemes, clubs, slogans and measures. There was cycling proficiency, Stop, Look and Listen and the Tufty Club. School playgrounds, like the one pictured, were marked out as highways with replica lights and beacons, and children obeyed the Highway Code as they pedalled along.

Right: Can you imagine going out for the day and ending up so close to a snake you can hear it hissing in your ear?, SSSS! SSSS! This little girl obviously could, as she can be seen bravely handling a snake at the zoo in Belle Vue Botanical Gardens. It was not everyone's idea of fun, but she was not a timid sort of child and she was made of sterner stuff than most of her chums. The zoo was giving visitors, of all ages, the chance to take a closer look at the sensational snakes and discover more about these fascinating reptiles. She was dressed like a proper lass. In 1946, girls wore skirts and donned ankle socks and went out on a summer's day with lightweight sandals on their feet. The young boy in the background was also kitted out in his very smart shorts and bared his knees to the world.

Above: Say, 'Cheese!' The kiddies were posing in their finery as they waited to take part in a Whit Sunday Walk in 1962. In other towns, the walks might be held on a Friday or Monday, but the essence was still the same. The local churches were the centres of attention and congregations paraded behind banners, often accompanied by brass bands. Children had new clothes to wear and usually called round at a relative's house after the event hoping to get something for their piggy banks. Some grumpy uncle complained that this was the only time in the year that his nephews and nieces ever showed their faces.

Right: It was time to play at Briscoe Lane Nursery School, Newton Heath, on a lovely summer's day in 1962. Surrounded by plenty of grass and open space, this was a grand place to be when the sun shone. The tiny paddling pool was ideal for cooling off and the teachers and nursery nurses provided a mixture of care and education that made it an ideal place from where to take the first tottering steps along the yellow brick road of education.

Clearly there is a difference of opinion as to who should become the next Tony McCoy or Hayley Turner, as these two youngers have a roadside disagreement on Cowesby Street, in 1968. One tearful lass was denied her turn on the metal rocking horse, probably by her elder brother, who is showing some style in the saddle, if being a little mean. Moss Side has had a vibrant history and there is no question of its contribution to the cultural life of Manchester. The Victorian terraced houses in Cowesby Street are part of a number in the Bowes Street area, currently being redeveloped as part of a £17m regeneration scheme.

Moss Side was a former rural township that became intensely urbanised during the Industrial Revolution. Migration from overseas in the 1950s helped to establish the hub of the city's Afro-Caribbean community. Families lived and played together. The quartet of youngsters on Bold Street in 1969, pictured above, included a girl who adopted a pose she had seen her mother use when at her most forthright. Many of the high rise flats, such as those in the background of the 1972 picture right, taken on Bishop Street, were demolished in the 1990s. The group have made an improvised tyre swing hanging from a tree branch. In an age before satellite tv and video games, children were happy to play outside all day, no matter how hot or cold it was. The regeneration of the housing and remodelling of the streets in the late 20th century helped make the area a more attractive place to be. Centres targeting the teens and twenties, focusing on education as well as recreation, are helping to offer acceptable outlets for youthful energy.

ON THE MOVE

nyone with even a passing knowledge of the city will instantly recognise the distinctive rise and sweep of this station approach. Until refurbishment in the earlier part of this century, the approach was the main access route to Piccadilly Station. Older readers will recall that it was known as London Road until 1960, though it started life in 1842 as Store Street and then Bank Top until it adopted the more familiar name in 1847. It has become the busiest of the city's stations and serves intercity routes across Great Britain. The taxi ranks, seen in the middle of this 1910 scene, were still there 90 years later. The road to the right, the old A6, now heads downhill towards the Mancunian Way or A57(M).

Right: Edwardian Deangsgate illustrated how old was vying with new. Electrically powered trams, stacked up in convoy, carried scores of people to and from the city, making the centre accessible to the residents of the suburbs who had previously to rely on walking or a bumpy ride in a horse drawn vehicle to get to the shops. At the same time, the gentry could still enjoy their personal carriage and driver as a means of transport. It would not have been quite right for them to take a seat alongside the lower classes in car 52. Look today from where Batchelor's showrooms for ladies' mantles and jackets once stood towards the Cathedral in the distance and your view will be dominated by multi-storey glass, steel and concrete structures, including the Renaissance Hotel on the left. The back of the Harvey Nicholls store is now in the distance to the right.

Below: Passengers on these horse drawn trams in Piccadilly might have enjoyed a glass or two in the Mosley and Albion Hotels before boarding. The cars were liberally covered with adverts for various household products, adding to Manchester Corporation's profits. In 1895, it had taken over the routes formerly administered by the Manchester Carriage and Tramways Company. Pictured in 1902, horses would be used for a further year until electrification of the tramway was completed.

Below: "Ello, ello, ello, what do we have here then"? is what this rather puzzled police officer might be saying to himself, as he stands on traffic duty in the centre of Manchester. The date is 17 February, 1937, and this tiny Rytecraft van, Britain's smallest, is travelling quietly along Deansgate. Powered by a 2 1/2 hp engine the van could travel 80 miles on a gallon of petrol, carry nearly 600 lbs and had a surprising top speed of 50mph. The vehicle was built by the British Motorboat Manufacturing Company, of Kings Cross, London, who were perhaps better known for building the British Rytecraft Scootacar between 1934-1940. They later changed the company name to BMB Engineering. Designed by Jack Shillan, the microcar originated as an electrically powered fair ground dodgem. Passengers on the tram must have looked on with open mouths as this tiny vehicle sped past, maybe with a delivery for 'The Borrowers'?

Above: Traffic at the junction of Oxford Street and Whitworth Street in 1924 demonstrates how quickly the number of vehicles on our roads increased after the 1914-18 War. This was particularly true for public service and goods vehicles as companies and corporations found alternative ways to the railways of moving people and products in bulk. The Palace Theatre continues to thrive as it has since opening in 1891, though its appearance has changed because of bomb damage during the last war and refurbishment in the late 1970s. The photograph was taken from Station Approach that leads up to Oxford Road Station.

Top right and right: In 1955, Market Street (right) was awash with both our legendary rain and the heavy traffic that came to blight this main shopping area. Car ownership

took off as we approached the latter half of the decade and Macmillan's 'never had it so good' era. Yet, when we examine the corresponding photograph (top right) from nearly half a century earlier, it would seem that a crowded thoroughfare was not a new phenomenon. Shoppers, traders, workers and visitors combined to make this older view just as frenetic as the more modern scene. Once known as Market Stead, this road was, until the later years of the 20th century, part of the old A6 road from Luton to Carlisle. Traffic flowed, when it could, and people strolled along the length of the street from Piccadilly down to St Mary's Gate. We used to get the bus into town to meet the boyfriend outside Lewis's, on the corner of Mosley Street. This was the department store where, as youngsters, we met Father Christmas and received a magic colouring book. As we got older and entered the decade known as

the Swinging 60s we would grab a quick drink in the Shakespeare on Fountain Street before heading off to the Three Coins a few yards further along the road. It was here, in January 1963, that we heard an up-and-coming group called the Beatles play. They were all right, but we liked the Hollies much better.

Manchester Airport and its terminal building were officially opened during a public air display on 25 June, 1938. Older readers will remember at the time the airport was called 'Ringway', after the parish it was within unitil 1975. Pre-war, KLM was the only international operator out of Ringway and offered a request stop at Doncaster. In its first 14 months, the airport handled around 7,600 passangers, which is a very modest number compared to the millions of people who fly out of

Manchester today. During World War II it was the location of RAF Ringway, and was important in the production and repair of military aircraft and training parachutists. The wartime years from 1940 to 1945 saw 60,000 of Britain's Airborne forces troops training there. Significantly to the war effort, some of the most famous military aircraft of the conflict were manufactured in Manchester. It was here that the prototype of the Lancaster bomber made its first flight. By 1960, the ordinary British holidaymaker started to show an interest in foreign travel. Package holidays to such glamorous spots as Spain and the Italian Riviera took the fancy of quite a few. At first it was a trickle, but by the end of the decade it had become a torrent as Blackpool gave way to Benidorm and Rhyl was abandoned in favour of Rimini. Looking east from its new tower across the airfield we can see that the place has yet to take on the look of an international hub. In peacetime, expansion was gradual, but business and, in particular, tourist travel demands of the 1960s and 1970s ensured that the site speeded up its evolution into an international airport.

AT WORK

Mr Martin, the poultry and greengrocer running this establishment proudly displays his prime irish chickens, turkeys and other fresh products for all to see. This was in Hightown in the 1920s, part of the Cheetham Hill district to the north of the city centre. Shop owners in this era had little regard for health and safety regulations. Today however, it's a different story with the insistence on sell-by dates and demands that we talk in grams and not ounces. It makes you wonder how we managed to win the war and survive into old age. Some of us have even picked up an apple we dropped on the floor, given it a polish on our sleeve, eaten it and lived to tell the tale.

Left: World War I was a terrible event, but at least it offered women an opportunity to show that they were perfectly capable of taking on many of the roles in the workplace that had been traditionally filled by men. When Kitchener pointed a finger from his recruitment poster and said that, 'Your country needs you', a jobs vacuum was created when men joined up. Women took their places with a determined spirit. The first two conductresses to work for the Tramways Department were proud to serve and do their bit.

Below: The Grange Laundry on Beech Road, Chorlton, was situated opposite the smithy. That guaranteed one good source of custom! In 1918, there were no such things as twin tubs, tumble driers or electric washing machines available to the ordinary housewife. However, this was quite an affluent area and those with some money to spare spurned the tedious job of washing clothes and paid for it to be done at a laundry. There were five such establishments in Chorlton alone, with another 275 or so dotted across the city around this time. A large steam powered engine ran a number of belt driven washing machines and the company also offered an iron service to finish off the job.

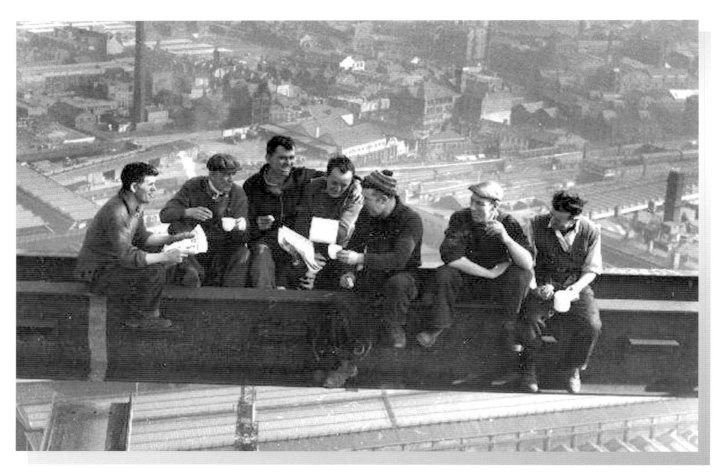

Above: At the time this photograph was taken in 1962, these daredevil workmen would be sitting as high off the ground as you could get, in the centre of Manchester, without being in an aeroplane. Unbelievably, they are nonchalantly perched on a steel beam some 387ft (118m) above the ground having a tea break and reading the paper. They are workmen constructing the CIS tower, which at the time of completion, was the tallest in the city and the second tallest office building outside London. The Grade II listed building on Miller Street remained the tallest until the 554ft (169m) Beetham Tower came along 44 years later.

Below: No, this is not a scene from Chicago during prohibition in the 1930s, or a shot of Eliot Ness in 'The Untouchables, it is actually Deansgate in Manchester. It would appear that representatives from Grimshaws could be taking delivery or just proudly showing off, the latest Chrysler Imperial motor car. The image is c1926 outside the Manchester city centre showroom, prior to them moving to a new depot at Chrysler House in Cateaton Street. By this time the automobile had firmly established itself as the newest and most popular method of road transport. The 1920s cars ushered a new automotive age. It didn't take long before they were enclosed and fitted with heaters to improve passenger comfort. By the end of the decade, cars had advanced in terms of style, speed and beauty with high levels of comfort and safety.

Glendale Foods - Innovation and Quality

The story of Glendale Foods Limited, based at Glendale House, Cobden Street, Salford, goes back to Frank Mortimer who in 1957 bought a butcher's shop on Lower Broughton Road, in Salford, for £1,700.

Frank's wife, Doris, also worked in the shop, whilst mother-in-law Molly looked after their children Gill, then aged six, and John, aged one.

By 1969, Frank and Doris were supplying industrial canteens such as Ward & Goldstone, British Aerospace and Ferranti. Soon there was not enough space, so they rented a unit in Pendleton in the old Mandleberg building. This part became 'Morties Meats'.

In 1972, daughter Gill joined the firm. Son John joined in 1974 after completing a Meat Technology course at Salford Technical College. The firm now began to produce reformed meat products such as beefburgers, grillsteaks and lamb grills, as well as cooking meats for others.

In 1991, Glendale introduced a two-pack frozen Doner Kebab product which was the first on the market. This led to a full range of microwaveable fast food snacks. By the late 1990s Glendale products were in most major supermarkets. The firm also won the hot food contract in Shell garages, which led to a range called 'Hot 1's'.

In 1998 the firm acquired the 'Yankee' brand from Freshbake - now Glendale's main snack brand. Two years later Glendale acquired all assets of a sausage company, and with the machinery that came with the deal entered the sausage market and increased cooking capacity by 400%.

In 2007 the firm merged with Supreme Foods Ltd and acquired The Great British Pudding Company.

Today, Glendale supplies many major meal manufacturers. Some 130 staff prepare over 80 tons of products every week, with annual sales exceeding £12 million.

Doris Mortimer worked in the butcher's shop until 1983. Frank continued to work for Glendale Foods in a consultant capacity until he was over 80.

The Glendale senior management team is now John Mortimer (Chairman), Paul Burkitt (Managing Director), Mark Jones (Operations Director), Gill Mortimer (HR Director) and Steve Revill (Company Secretary).

There is still a butcher's shop on Lower Broughton Road that has the name Frank Mortimer over the door – a reminder that from tiny acorns mighty oaks can grow.

Top: Founder, Frank Mortimer and his wife, Doris. **Centre left:** The first delivery van. **Left:** The area of the original shop was redeveloped and moved to Mocha Parade but such was the reputation that when Frank sold the shop the new owner (pictured) kept the name. **Above:** Glendale Foods Directors 2012. L-R: Mark Jones, Paul Burkitt, Gill Mortimer, Steve Revill and John Mortimer.

F Duerr & Sons Ltd
A Family Business Since 1881

Duerr's is the oldest family-owned jam maker in England. Now based in Floats Road Wythenshawe, Manchester, in the glorious North West, they've been making quality preserves to their family recipes for over 130 years.

In 1872, Fred Duerr, then aged 24, married Mary Eva Naylor, aged 16. In her small kitchen in Heywood, Mary made jams and marmalades for her husband, family and friends to enjoy. Their reputation for quality was well known within the locality. Fred, originally a leather-dresser by trade, was moving up the career ladder and had just started to work as a grocery commission agent in Heywood.

In 1881, Fred met with a buyer from the Heywood Co-operative Society who was experiencing difficulty in obtaining jams of high quality. There were no laws at that time about honest and complete food labelling, and all kinds of unsavoury 'fillers' were being put into the jam he was being offered. The buyer had heard of Mary's jams and asked if Fred would consider supplying the Co-op. (These days, one hopes, he would have asked Mary!)

From that chance meeting the family business was born. At first Mary did all the cooking in the family kitchen, and Fred delivered the jams to the Heywood Co-op in a handcart. Business flourished as demand grew, until manufacturing premises were required.

Fred raised the capital to build and equip a small factory at Deanhead, Guide Bridge, Manchester. A publication of 1890, 'Century's Progress', described it: "Every part is filled up in thorough style with plant and apparatus of the latest and most improved description." Here Fred joined his young wife in the full time production of preserves.

Fred was a member of the Corn Exchange which he attended every Tuesday. He attributed his success to careful fruit buying and the application of scientific principles to jam making.

In 1890 the Duerr's manufacturing needs outgrew their Guide Bridge premises and Fred commissioned a purpose-built factory on Prestage Street,

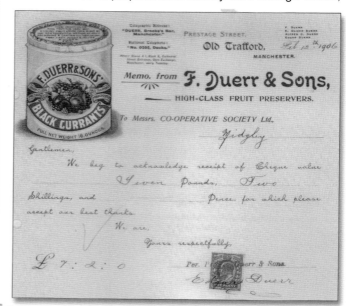

Top: Fred Duerr who founded the business and his wife, Mary Duerr, who provided the recipes and the inspiration for the family business. Left: A 1993 picture of Duerr's first factory. Above: The company's earliest letter heading dated 12th February, 1906.

Oliver managed the administrative work and finance.

Alfred took control of selling and building up a steady trade with many different co-operative societies in the North West.

Innovation and quality have always been the cornerstone of Duerr's philosophy. The firm pioneered vacuum sealing in 1905 when many competitors were still using cardboard caps and paper tissues until the 1950s! The company managed to survive two world wars and the depression and continue to grow from strength to strength.

Fred's youngest son Edgar was something of an inventor with an enthusiasm for the new fangled motor cars – being prosecuted in 1910 for breaking the speeding limit of 12 miles an hour! Edgar came

Old Trafford. He employed Mr A Pearson to do the work which cost him £1,315 16s 4d to build. This did not include the cost of manufacturing equipment which he had made to the highest standards.

In 1903, Duerr's spent the sizeable sum of £148 on a new Cornish boiler, installed by J K & R Lord, of Bury. Then, in 1906, Fred had a telephone system installed in time for the busy summer fruit season.

The firm was well known and well appreciated for the generous wages it paid to its staff. Hard work was expected in return, but time was found to take them on works outings to Blackpool to enjoy the funfair and donkey rides. The women in the factory wore long starched aprons. When times were hard in their personal lives, Duerr's were supportive, and this too was not taken for granted. The workers knew when they were well off and most of them served the company for many years. Perhaps Mrs Emily Deakin holds the record, going to work for Duerr's at the age of 14 and finally retiring at 74.

Fred Duerr took his three of his sons, Oliver, Edgar and Alfred, into the family business.

into his own during the First World War. During the Boer War, Duerr's had sent out tins of jam to the Lancashire Fusiliers, but in 1914 the company completely changed direction and put its expertise into manufacturing to support the war effort.

Top left: Staff take to donkeys on a staff trip to Blackpool in 1905. **Above:** A group of women employees in their long starched aprons pictured in 1910. **Left:** L-R Oliver Duerr, Edgar Duerr and Alfred Duerr, sons of the founder. **Right:** A 1914 advert for Duerr's high class preserves.

Edgar invented and patented a collapsible pocket periscope for use by soldiers in the deadly trench warfare. The periscopes were extremely sturdy and were responsible for saving many lives. Duerr's was also the first company to use tamper-evident 'button caps' and shrink sleeving on its range of products.

Fred Duerr died in 1917. The firm was incorporated as a limited company in 1924. By 1935 Oliver's sons, Norman and Clive Duerr, had taken over the running of the business. Norman concentrated on administration and engineering whilst Clive was the salesman.

During the Second World War Norman Duerr ran the factory. It was a period of constant struggle to obtain the strictly-rationed sugar and other raw materials. Before the days of easy freezing, all fruit, of course, had to be processed immediately which made planning difficult. There were also labour shortages as skilled workers were conscripted.

Spare parts and machinery were in short supply even when the war was long over.

Alfred Duerr's son Harry rejoined the form in 1947 after serving in the army. He quickly established himself as a successful fruit buyer. It was nothing for him to be at Smithfield Market, in Manchester, at four in the morning to select the pick of the fruit – or at eight in the evening and be in the middle of a field inspecting produce.

Norman's son, Tony Duerr, joined the family business full time in 1960 after coming down from Cambridge University. Later that same year Clive Duerr retired through ill health at the age of just 51.

When Chairman Edgar Duerr died in 1962, at the age of 82, he was succeeded by Norman Duerr. Sadly, Norman passed away in 1964, at the age of just 57.

Jim Harrison, who had married Edgar Duerr's daughter, Alma, became Non-Executive Chairman in 1965.

At the same time Tony Duerr was appointed Managing Director, age 27, and inherited

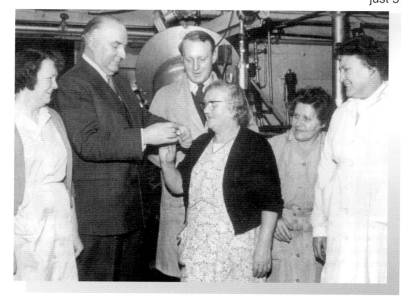

Top right: A selection of vacuum sealed jars, pioneered by Fred Duerr in 1905. **Centre left:** Third generation, L-R: Harry Duerr, Clive Duerr and Norman Duerr. **Left:** Norman Duerr and Tony Duerr present a gold watch to Emily Deakin who commenced her employment with Duerr's at the age of 14 and retired at the age of 74. **Above right:** Former Chairman of Duerr's, Jim Harrison.

To cope with the ever-increasing demands for storage and production, in 1996 the company invested in a new warehouse and second production site in Wythenshawe. The 70,000 square feet site houses all the raw materials, together with the finished product. In 1997 Duerr's completed the installation of a specialist production line in order to satisfy demand for a new range of jams in which more whole fruit pieces were retained in the finished product.

By 2001, Duerr's main customers were the major multiples; its products were not just sold in the north but all over the

the running of a business that was 50% wholesale and 50% with Co-operative societies - and a policy of refusing to supply multiples!

The early 1960s were a very difficult time in the business as Duerr's wholesale customers got together in groups such as Spar, Mace and VG. As a consequence Duerr's lost a lot of its wholesale distribution, and some shareholders were in favour of closing down the business when turnover fell to just £200,000.

Two important events, however, occurred which gave the company a much needed boost. Firstly, in the late 1960s Duerr's secured the contract to pack V.G Preserves, thereby, increasing its volume by 50%. Later, in the early 1970s, the biggest leap forward the company had experienced came when Bill Postlethwaite and David Owen of Kwik Save put Duerr's products onto their shelves and helped make Duerr's the national brand that it is today.

In 1989, the company diversified from its mainstream jam and marmalade production by entering the peanut butter market. A new, purpose-built peanut butter production line was installed at Prestage Street, and Duerr's started to supply the major multiples with crunchy and smooth varieties under their own label, the Duerr brand and the Whole Earth brand of peanut butter.

country and overseas. Some 90% of Duerr's trade is now with the multiples and its products are sold with the Duerr's label and also under multiples' own 'Private Labels'. Products made in Wythenshawe can be found in Asda, Kwik Save, Sainsburys, Safeway, Tesco, Waitrose and Morrisons as well as Hong Kong, Saudi Arabia, Australia, the Faroe Islands, France, USA, Greece, Ireland, Gambia, Singapore, Malaysia, Japan, Italy, Denmark and China.

In the last 50 years Duerr's has expanded to such an extent that it is now one of the country's top three jam manufacturers (and the largest 'independent') with a 15%

*Top left and above: Then and now views of methods used in the jam production area. **Left:** The new livery in 1995.*

Throughout its existence the company has been generous to many charities. Perhaps the most unusual event happened in 1989 when Tony Duerr, with the aid of an aircraft and seven friends, raised ten thousand pounds for charity by playing four full rounds of golf in Scotland, Ireland, Wales and England in one day, beginning at four in the morning and finishing at ten o'clock at night.

share of the market, and with its production line for peanut butter, started only in 1989, it had captured 30% of the peanut butter market. By 2002 the company was filling around 500,000 items each day, and enjoying an annual turnover of about £28 million.

2010 saw the end of an era. After 115 years at Prestage Street production was moved to a new purpose-built peanut butter factory in Dallimore Road, just 100 yards from their Wythenshawe site. There still remain's a connection with Prestage Street however, as the site now is now home to a new Housing Association project who, in honour of the company's history in the area, named one of the new roads 'Duerrs Drive'.

Duerr's market share has steadily increased over the years as the company's reputation for quality jams, marmalades and peanut butter has grown. Today, Duerr's products can be found all over the world as the company exports to almost thirty countries; the firm now has 200 employees and annual turnover of £50 million.

In 2010, The Duerr's 'Lady Marmalade Ball', in aid of Wythenshawe Hospital, caused donations to flood in. The £20,000 raised went towards the hospital's One in an Million Appeal to raise £1 million to help refurbish the antenatal facilities and maternity unit at Wythenshawe Hospital.

The following year the Duerr's 'Preserved on Film Ball 2011' raised another £22,000 for the same cause.

In the previous ten years Duerr's had raised no less than £500,000 for charities – not least the £8,000 Mark and Richard Duerr raised on a sponsored event, bicycling from London to Paris in 2009.

Top left: *Duerr's new peanut butter site at Dallimore Road, completed in September 2010.* **Above:** *During 2001 and early 2002 the company moved its offices from Old Trafford to Floats Road in Wythenshawe. The new offices pictured contained a canteen which was capable of serving the staff 24 hours a day, seven days a week.* **Left:** *Duerr's staff receiving their Food Hygiene certificates. The staff had a 100% pass rate.*

Meanwhile, as well as helping the local hospital, Duerr's has gone into the 'healthcare' business itself, recently launching Ulmo Active 10+ in the UK, a new Chilean 'super honey', which is clinically proven to kill the bacteria that is associated with coughs and sore throats. Ulmo honey is antimicrobial, meaning that it encompasses antibacterial properties (a renowned health benefit of Manuka honey) – and also fights virus and fungi.

Of course, one first has to get the lid off the jar! A new innovation for glass jar lids is bringing welcome relief to anyone who relies on tea towels, hot water or a strong partner every time they are faced with opening a jar of their favourite preserve.

Duerr's has introduced the innovative OrbitTM lid across its range of jams and marmalades nationwide following a successful trial in stores.

Response to the new lids has been overwhelmingly positive. The simple mechanism, developed by Crown Holdings Inc., a world leader in metal packaging, reduces the effort required to get the jar open. The appearance of the lid is very similar to a normal twist-off lid, but it is actually in two parts: a central panel is sealed to the jar by vacuum, and an outer ring is screwed in place. Twisting firstly loosens the ring, then smoothly pushes the panel away from the jar to break the seal. In this way, the ring acts as a tool to break the seal.

It is likely that the speed of change in the industry will accelerate, but the company, with its heavy investment in the latest technology and skilled personnel, is enjoying meeting the challenges of the 21st century. All employees have taken, and passed, a course in Food Hygiene.

F Duerr & Son Ltd remains very much a family business and a member of the Duerr family has led the company since its inception. Tony Duerr who officially retired in 1997 remains Chairman and his two sons Mark and Richard run the business, presiding over the new factory in Wythenshawe. Such continuity has ensured that the traditions lovingly begun by Fred and Mary Duerr so long ago continues to be adhered to today, with the emphasis still on high quality ingredients, innovation and manufacturing excellence.

Top left: *Duerr's honey processing plant.* **Left:** *A selection of Duerr's products.* **Bottom left:** *Tony Duerr presents a £10,000 cheque to charity after playing four rounds of golf in England, Scotland, Ireland and Wales in one day.* **Below:** *Tony Duerr being presented with a claret jug by his sons, Mark and Richard, on the the day he celebrated 40 years with the company.*

Stax - A Supa Trader

With its flagship branch and head office in Holloway Drive, Manchester, Stax Trade Centres plc is the biggest non-food cash and carry wholesale trade supplier in the country. Stax has been supplying the trade for over three decades and has a wealth of expertise in knowing exactly what trade customers want and need.

The firm stocks more than 40,000 product lines. The range includes Tools and Hardware, Building and Joinery, DIY, Electrical and Lighting, Plumbing and Heating, Kitchens and Bathrooms, Decorating, Outdoor and Gardening and much more.

Stax has grown organically over the years and now turns over in excess of £100m in annual sales. The company has five warehouse branches up to 100,000 square feet in size, located in Manchester, Birmingham, Leeds, Bristol and, most recently in a new Edinburgh trade centre. In 2011 Stax also strengthened its delivery arm with the acquisition of Edinburgh based delivered wholesale trade supplier DF Wishart & Co Ltd.

It was in 1981 that Stax Manchester began trading. By 1985 turnover had topped £4 million. The following year Eddie Brady and David Hibbert acquired the business from Maccess in a management buy-out.

The original Stax Trade Centre goes back to a cash and carry wholesale business set up by Maccess, the motor parts distributor, back in 1981. Two Stax sites, Manchester and Leeds, opened that year. Another branch opened in Tottenham, North London, in 1983.

Despite increasing the range of goods sold to include bulk chemicals, catering equipment, ceramic tiles, furniture and office stationery the business failed to thrive. All three sites were in the red and the decision was taken to close Tottenham in December 1984. The head office in Leeds was also closed leaving just two branches, each with a high degree of autonomy.

The Manchester branch was left to be run by Eddie Brady, who had been the branch manager there since its opening in 1981. In 1984, on the closure of the Tottenham branch and subsequently the Leeds head office, David Hibbert was transferred to Manchester to work with Eddie with the responsibility for negotiating business terms and marketing.

Under Eddie and David the Manchester branch began to flourish as they exercised their autonomy, pioneering what would become the well known Stax formula of keen

Top: *David Hibbert - Joint Managing Director, and Eddie Brady - Chairman and Joint Managing Director.* ***Left:*** *A view of the interior of Stax, Manchester, on the occasion of it's opening in 1981.*

per cent to reach £4.2 million and a £250,000 loss in 1984 was transformed into a healthy profit in 1986.

Everything seemed to be going well until, in September 1987, exactly a year after the management buy-out, disaster struck and the premises in Wardley Industrial Estate burned to the ground.

In the early hours of the morning of September 18 a fire started at the site which rapidly grew into a blaze. Within the space of a couple of hours the blaze was an inferno. By the time the fire brigade had been alerted by local residents and arrived in Holloway Drive the roller shutter doors to the site were white hot. Within 30 minutes of the fire brigade being on the scene the overhead power lines melted and had fallen onto nearby houses; this forced the firemen to withdraw until the power could be cut giving the fire even more time to take hold.

The smoke was so intense it was affecting traffic on the nearby M62 (now M60)

By the time Eddie Brady and David Hibbert arrived most of the business was engulfed and they had to watch as their new venture went up in flames. Surveying the wreckage the next day both David and Eddie were devastated by the smoking ruin of their business. However, once they had rid themselves of the flock of loss adjusters touting for business, the pair set about rebuilding their company.

Fortunately, a warehouse on Shield Drive, on the same industrial estate,

pricing and regular promotions on a comprehensive range of products stocked in depth. Despite that triumph in Manchester, however, the Leeds branch continued to lose money. Maccess decided to close it and Eddie and David grasped the opportunity to-buy out the Manchester branch.

The first suggestion of a management buy-out had been mooted in 1985 but was given added impetus when Maccess itself was subject to a management buy-out from Burmah Oil for £10.5 million. One month later, in September 1986, Eddie and David, helped financially by non-executive director Graham Gardiner, negotiated a £750,000 buy-out from Maccess that resulted in the formation of Stax Trade Centres Ltd.

It was a big gamble. Both Eddie, who now became Chairman and Joint Managing Director, and David, his co-Joint Managing Director, had to take out second mortgages on their homes to help finance the project. That year Stax had moved into profit. Over two years sales increased at an annual average rate of 25

Top left: From left to right; David Shore and Ken Widdowson, of Maccess, receive the final payment from Eddie Brady and David Hibbert in 1987. Above left: Ken Dodd with Eddie Brady, at the official opening of Stax, Manchester in 1981. Below: Stax, Manchester, as it looked in the early 1980s.

though only two thirds of the size as the one destroyed, was vacant and they were able to move the business into it. Stax tills started to ring again on 22 November, 1987, just nine weeks from the date of the fire.

While trading continued from the temporary site, construction work began on a new building. In January 1988, the foundations of the new Manchester store were laid and nine months later Stax Manchester reopened - exactly a year to the day of the fire.

That same year Stax was able to open a Birmingham depot at Smethwick, in the West Midlands. Within 12 months sales would top £10 million.

Having seen the original Leeds branch close in the 1980s Eddie and David now opened a new Leeds branch in 1992. Stax would go on to acquire its close rival W E Merris, in Birmingham, in 1995, and the following year the 52,000 sq ft Bristol branch of Stax would open.

Meanwhile, back in the North West, in November 1996, Manchester was the first Stax branch to take over £100,000 in a single day.

In 1997, Stax rescued Liverpool-based Domcraft Ltd from the receiver and re-launched the delivered wholesaler as Dompak-Grosvenor Ltd, a subsidiary company of the Stax plc Group.

In Manchester, business continued to grow and in March 1997 the footings were laid for a new extension; by the end of August that year the new -ook Manchester was opened despite the challenge of floods in the Timber and Building section, burst pipes in the car park meant no water for the kitchen and toilets and staff having to troop down the road to use other facilities and, for a while, no gas or heating. One million pounds was invested in the

Top and above: *The aftermath of the devastating fire that occurred in 1988.* ***Left:*** *Stax Trade Centre following refurbishment after the fire.*

extension, increasing space by over a third. Not only did Stax have to buy out its next door neighbour but, because the site was some 18 feet higher than the existing store, the removal of the excess land alone would cost over £160,000 for the excavations in order to add an extra 14,000 sq ft to the existing 38,000 sq ft warehouse.

Expansion continued elsewhere too. Stax bought the Woodside brand in 1998. By 1999 turnover topped £59 million helped by opening on Saturdays for the first time.

In the year 2000 Stax launched its Supa range, SupaValue and the Stax and Supa websites.

A programme called SupaValue gave customers marketing materials to promote their shops and help grow their own sales. The programme started with just 10 retailers and has grown to over 150 regular participants with millions of promotional leaflets being printed every year.

Stax also made the headlines when in April of 2000 some of the company's staff came face to face with masked robbers who had entered the building, but being confronted by courageous staff the robbers had to flee empty handed.

In 2001, a new Birmingham depot opened and turnover reached £70 million whilst Dompak moved from Liverpool to new premises in Widnes. From a turnover of £2.5 million in 1981

sales had grown every single year, slowly at first reaching just £15 million in 1991 before rapidly taking off to reach that staggering £70 million at the start of the new millennium.

In April 2005, Stax sold its wholesale delivery division, Dompak Grosvenor, allowing the group to better focus on its core business of wholesale cash and carry. A brand new, purpose-built 78,000 sq ft Stax Leeds cash and carry trade centre opened in the following year.

Stax had significantly expanded the Supa range including SupaDec, its range of decorating products, then SupaTool, its range of hand and power tools. 2007 saw the launch of more SupaHome and SupaLite electrical products and a big new range of SupaGarden gardening products. The range, which started as a few gardening lines, reached over 2,000 products and is now a major brand in the DIY market valued at over £30 million.

Stax also launched several major marketing catalogues towards the

Top and inset: Graham Gardiner opening the Bristol branch in 1996, inset, and David Hibbert and Eddie Brady with Sharon Davies on the same occasion, top. Left: An aerial view of Stax, Manchester following the extension in 1997.

end of the decade. 2007 saw the launch of a giant Trade brochure and a Kitchens and Bathrooms catalogue, 2008 its first major Gardening publication, and annual Supa Catalogues and Outdoor Living catalogues.

Sales meanwhile continued to grow and by 2007 had reached £80.8 million. And then the biggest Stax project ever was unveiled.

In October 2007, Stax announced it was to build a massive new flagship branch and head office in Manchester, literally across the road from its existing Manchester branch on the site of the old Convoys warehousing operation. Stax was to invest over £11 million in the largest single project it had ever undertaken, Chairman Eddie Brady said: "Our Manchester operation continues to be our busiest and over the past year we have been looking to find a suitable site to build a brand new state-of-the-art warehouse. I am delighted to announce that we completed the purchase and our plan is to move into the new premises in the autumn of 2009."

But the economic crash of 2008 put all plans in jeopardy. Should any firm risk investing so much capital in such uncertain times? Only a firm with real confidence in its future would do so. Stax went ahead.

Customers and staff of Stax existing branch would have no difficulty in finding the new branch directly opposite the entrance to the existing branch. At over 100,000 sq ft, the new purpose-built branch would virtually double the size of the existing Manchester branch. The store has 50% more selling bays, four

times the current storage capacity, a purpose-built showroom, a separate goods in area and a 200-space car park with extra large spaces.

On 1 September, 2009, Stax opened the doors of its magnificent, massive new flagship branch and head office in Holloway Drive, Manchester. The store launched amidst a flurry of excitement and promotional activity including Stax largest ever Marketing Campaign, including three months of radio advertising, billboards, and celebrity opening

Above and left: David Hibbert (third from left), Eddie Brady (second right of Ken Dodd) and staff welcome Ken Dodd back to Stax to open the new flagship branch in 2009. *Below:* Interior view of Stax Trade Center in 2012.

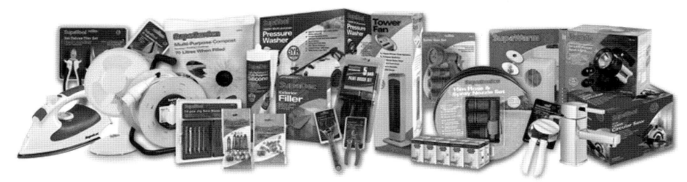

by the legendary comedian Ken Dodd who returned to Stax 28 years after opening the original Stax Manchester.

The decade has seen the emergence of online activity affecting every area of communication, and in 2011 Stax launched an impressive new website.

That same month Stax announced the acquisition of Edinburgh based D F Wishart Ltd. Wishart turned over £6-7 million per annum and was a long-established family business, whose product range complemented Stax. The acquisition strengthened Stax's delivered business, helped with the growth of the garden sector business and the expansion of the Supa brand into Scotland.

Meanwhile, following the success of Supa, which now includes over 3,000 lines, the company extended its range of own-branded products. The new SP range introduced in 2012 features a new bathroom range. Ambassador is a new range of garden tools and Picardy a brand of hand tools and fixings. Finally the brand Glenwear is a professional range of workwear.

In September 2011, in Edinburgh, Stax opened its fifth Cash and Carry depot. Stax Chairman Eddie Brady said: "This is our first branch in Scotland and in my home city of Edinburgh, so I'm very pleased to bring Stax 'home' and to support the independent retailers of the region".

Stax celebrated its 30th anniversary in September 2011 by reporting an annual turnover which had reached almost £100 million.

And it was not just sales that had grown. In the years since its founding staff numbers had increased from 50 to over 600. Staff who joined the firm as general assistants on the shop floor could, with hard work and commitment, become senior managers within the group. As well as Eddie and David, other members of staff who were with the company from its foundation and who have witnessed the spectacular growth are Tim Ball, Della Butler, Ali Djabarouti, Lynda Brooks, Sue Hoben and Mark Hallows.

The growth of Stax has been remarkable, but nothing would have been possible without Eddie Brady and David Hibbert who bravely risked their all back in 1986.

Above: *A selection of products from Stax's Supa range.*
Below: *Exterior view of Stax Trade Centre in Holloway Drive, Manchester, 2012.*

The Morson Group
Delivering Skills, Applying Expertise

Morson's corporate head office is just a stone's throw away from its original location in Eccles where Group Chairman, Ged Mason's father, Gerry, first started an engineering recruitment business in 1969. According to Gerry: "When I founded Morson I never set any targets; just the burning ambition to be the best in our sector, trusting that passion and ambition coupled with integrity would be the driving force for success."

Morson International was founded by Gerry Mason to offer technical staffing solutions to the Engineering industry. It now generates approximately 92% of the Morson Group Plc turnover and has 425 employees. The Salford head office now houses the core recruitment teams and support departments including payroll, accounts, administration, systems compliance, business development and operations management.

8% of the Group's turnover is generated by Morson Projects, which employs more than 750 Morson Projects personnel, housed within modern, fully equipped offices and   utilising the latest technology. The company offers a compatible and complementary service to Morson's clients.

Founded in Salford in 1969, Morson Group plc is now one of the region's largest businesses. The Group is comprised of Morson International, which provides specialist engineering and technical personnel, and Morson Projects Limited, which provides outsourced engineering and project management design services. Core markets include Aerospace, Energy and Rail with further expertise across IT, Telecoms, Oil and Gas, Scientific, Automotive and Construction.

Ged Mason, the Group's CEO says: "Manchester has always been a fantastic place to conduct business. From our first office at our family home on New Lane, Salford, to our corporate headquarters at Adamson House, on Centenary Way, Trafford Park, we have enjoyed working within the diverse and exciting business culture Manchester provides."

The Morson Group has been established for more than 40 years, beginning as a small, family run business and growing into an international Plc. The following provides a timeline of key events:

From 1960 Gerry Mason worked as a self-employed Mechanical Design draughtsman and found working for different companies on assignment a challenge which suited his temperament.

Top left: Founder, Gerry Mason, today's Non Executive Chairman (seated) and son Ged Mason, CEO of the Morson Group PLC pictured in 1996. *Left:* The working environment in the mid-1990s. *Above:* The Morson Group policy is to consistently provide efficient and effective solutions to their vast client base. The management system complies with the requirements of EN ISO 9001:2008.

In the late 1960s, Gerry was offered a contract to open and manage a new branch office for a Contract Design Organisation in Toronto, Canada, which he found exciting and a great learning opportunity in management and business development.

After three years in Canada, Gerry returned with his family to the UK having gained valuable experience. He believed that he could take the new knowledge of how the North Americans operated and bring something new to the Design Agency Business. As a result Gerry founded J Morson & Co Ltd (which was Morson's original name).

The company, founded by Gerry on 10 September 1969, provided engineers, designers and draftsman on temporary assignments to various industry sectors throughout the UK. The first placement was a structural engineer assigned to ICI in Runcorn, Cheshire. Soon larger contracts were obtained, not least one at Ashmore, Benson & Pease for 30-plus piping and mechanical designers. Gerry would eventually put the company on the map with upwards of 500 contractors. Apart from the usual challenges of starting a new business, with little funding, and breaking into a sector dominated by several established and fairly large competitors, Gerry soon put his stamp on the sector.

An early challenge was the postal strike of 1971, which these days wouldn't matter so much with the advancement of technology. However, back then the Morson contract design engineers working all over the UK were paid via posted cheques or postal orders (there were no BACS/bank transfer facilities then) and some contractors didn't even have a bank account. Gerry and his staff drove all over the country to hand deliver wages in order to retain the company's credibility and demonstrate the value the company placed on its personnel - this routine lasted for seven weeks.

*Above: Training in progress in 1996. **Below:** A selection of sectors in the Morson portfolio.*

Asset Condition Surveys

Nuclear Engineering

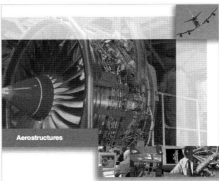

Aerostructures

Mechanical Engineering

Switchgear, Power, CE&I

NC, Planning & CMM

Another challenge came when legislation changed twice with regard to self-employed design draughtsmen. For National Insurance purposes contractors were now deemed employees and the NI payment was increased, whereas for Income Tax contractors were still deemed self-employed (a stranger bureaucratic contradiction). Some two years later the income tax authority adopted the same interpretation. This resulted in Morson changing their whole approach to dealing with contractors.

1979 saw significant development with the founding of sister company Morson Projects, a Design Engineering and Project Management company which grew the business from a recruitment agency to a multi-disciplined organisation. For over 30 years Morson Projects has provided multi-disciplined engineering, project management and design services to clients within the Energy, Utilities, Aerospace, Infrastructure, Telecoms and General Engineering sectors. The services provided range from basic detailing exercises through to complete 'turn-key' project management services.

The steady growth of the Group to become the leading engineering and design organisation in its sector is, according to Gerry, largely down to loyal staff. He was also fortunate enough to have an understanding, supportive wife, and a son who has shown enthusiasm and the same passion he had to take the business forward with honesty and integrity. This is essentially the hallmark of a family run business; that employees are treated with compassion and fairness.

In 1990, Morson brought the 'Managed Service' recruitment model to Britain. The first such contract was with British Energy and, over two decades later, Morson still manages this contract. Over the past 22 years, Morson has evolved this model, working with clients to develop tailored solutions that meet all of their resourcing needs.

During the 1990s and early 2000s, Morson continued to grow, winning contracts that enabled the company to branch out into the IT, Telecoms and Scientific sectors, whilst strengthening core areas such as Aerospace, Energy and Rail.

The Morson Group was joined by Paul Gilmour, Financial Director, in 1993 and Dr. Kevin Gorton, now Managing Director, in 1995. Under the leadership of Gerry, Ged, Paul and Kevin, the company continued to flourish.

Top: Two ISO 9001s that have been awarded to the Morson Group. *Above:* Morson directors at the London Stock Exchange on the company's first day of flotation, 2006. *Below left:* In 2008 Morson Projects and Yacht Teccon signed a Letter of Intent to strengthen pan-European positioning in engineering services. *Below:* The signing of contracts in 2009 as Morson Projects secured a three year preferred supply agreement contract with EADS, a global leader in aerospace, defence and related services.

In 1999 Ged Mason led the sale of a majority stake to Barclays Private Equity, which was followed in 2005 by the subsequent buy back. In 2006, the Morson Group Plc floated on the AIM market, in an oversubscribed flotation at a share price of £1.60. Following its flotation, Morson has continued its trend of year on year growth and expanded services both organically and via acquisitions.

In 2007, these acquisitions included Westbury, White & Nunn, Pentagon Personnel and CTS.

In 2009, Morson celebrated its 40th anniversary and opened international offices in Colombia and Australia.

2010 brought significant change, with the integration of Morson International and Morson Projects at a purpose-built Head Office facility on Centenary Way, in Salford.

Two more acquisitions were made in 2010; Acetech and Wynnwith. The Wynnwith acquisition brought with it an additional office presence in Milan, Italy, which increased the Group's capabilities within the European Aerospace market. Morson also opened offices in Germany and Brazil, further strengthening the global activity of the company.

In 2011, the Group surpassed £500million turnover; another record breaking year. During 2011 Morson expanded further both nationally and internationally, opening new offices in Bristol, Aberdeen and Johannesburg, South Africa. The Group also created a new service sector, 'People Flow', and gained the ISO 14001 accreditation at its Head Office building; a demonstration of its ongoing commitment to the environment.

Today a multi-million pound enterprise, the Morson Group has 32 offices placed strategically throughout the UK, and international representation in nine global locations.

Top: The company's former Stableford Hall, Eccles, head office. *Left:* In 2009 Morson International were highly commended at the Recruiter Awards for Excellence. *Below:* The Morson Group management team, L-R: Dr Kevin Gorton, Ged Mason, Paul Gilmour, Gerry Mason and Ian Knight.

Given that the business is now operating on a global scale, the question often asked is why is it based in Salford? According to Gerry it is "simply because I was born in the area, and back then there was a pool of talented engineers and designers in the North West. The people were all hard working and honest, therefore I saw no reason to move our headquarters - although we did open branch offices in various regions throughout the UK, USA, Canada and Kuwait."

With a dominant presence in Salford and demonstrated growth, it is no wonder that the Morson Group won the Salford Business of the Year Award 2011.

In addition to the business success experienced by Morson, the company is also a contributor to the local community, with ongoing commitments to local charities such as 'Destination Florida' and to two 'official' charities which change on a yearly basis.

Destination Florida is an Eccles based, North West charity which provides children with severe and sometimes terminal illnesses the opportunity to go to Florida for a week to visit Disney World and Universal Studios. The Morson Group CEO Ged Mason is heavily involved with this charity and frequently travels with the children on these 'holidays of a lifetime'. Ged's work with the charity is greatly appreciated. Ann Billington, the Fundraising Manager for 'Destination Florida', says: "As a trustee, Ged is a loyal and committed supporter of the children's charity. Not only does Ged accompany the children's trip to Disneyland as a carer but also gives generously and

supports many fundraising events. The charity is enriched by people such as Ged giving their time and support."

It is Ged and Gerry's leading example that encourages the Morson Group employees to promote awareness and to continue fundraising on a continuous basis.

Morson selects two 'official' charities every year. These are nominated and voted for by Morson Group employees and finalised by the charity committee. The company aims to include one national and one North West regional charity each year and arranges fundraising activities such as

sponsored runs and raffles so that a significant donation can be made to each charity once the 12 month sponsorship has been completed.

An avid sports fan, Ged Mason supports a range of sports from football (a diehard Manchester United supporter) to horse racing.

Several years ago Ged happened to be in the Midland Hotel on St Patrick's Day when a well-known Greater Manchester businessman - the late Tim Kilroe - and his family walked in carrying the Gold Cup they had won earlier that day at the Cheltenham Festival.

Top left: Morson charity 2010 cheque presentation to North West Air Ambulance, one of the many charities to benefit from fundraising events organised by the company and its staff over the years. ***Above:*** Gerry Mason hands over the 'key' to a new minibus donated to the Seashell Trust in 2009. ***Far left and left:*** A certificate of Assessment awarded to the Morson group PLC in 2011 (left) and the ISO 14001 Environmental Management System certificate gained in October 2011 (left).

From this initial introduction, Ged was hooked and is now part-owner of four horses which are stabled with champion national hunt trainer Paul Nicholls, including Sporazene, which won the final race in the 2004 Cheltenham Festival and the Irish Champion Hurdle. Ged says: "Some owners go their whole lives without ever having a winner, but it has been my good fortune to have 30 since I started racing in 2000."

Ged now owns a number of horses with his friend Sir Alex Ferguson, including 'What A Friend', which finished in 4th place in the Cheltenham Gold Cup, 2011. Never deterred from a challenge, Ged is still chasing the dream of winning the Gold Cup with 'What a Friend' in 2012's Cheltenham Festival, following continued improvement since last year's closely run race.

So what motivates this remarkable business to keep on winning? According to its founder, Morson Group Chairman Gerry Mason, unlike horseracing:

"There is no finish line, and that is the challenge"

Top left, bottom and right: *Ged Mason (right) is pictured with Sir Alex Ferguson (left), Manager of Manchester United and Salford Artist Harold Riley, as they officially open Adamson House, pictured below and right.* **Above:** *What a Friend takes the last fence on his way to victory in the Totesport Bowl at Aintree in 2011.*

Manchester High School for Girls
Today's Students, Tomorrow's Successful Women

Manchester High School for Girls was founded in 1874 as a result of the work of the Manchester Association for the Promotion of the Education of Women. At that time there was widespread suspicion of female education. Girls were regarded as intellectually inferior to boys and there were fears that education for girls might damage their health, would undermine social norms, and be an unnecessary extra burden on the taxpayer. Despite these fears a public subscription was launched in Manchester to establish a girls' school "of the highest type" and over a hundred Mancunians contributed sums ranging from £1 to £150.

Famous people

The character of Manchester High School has been reflected in the quality of its pupils. Emmeline Pankhurst chose to send her three daughters Christabel (attended 1893-1897), Sylvia (attended 1893-1898) and Adela (attended 1893-1902) to

MHSG. Dorothy Hale (attended 1904-1911) was the first woman journalist to work on the Manchester Guardian and the Manchester Evening News, whilst C P Scott, the editor of the then Manchester Guardian, was a school governor (1875-1888).

In the arts, the soprano Isobel Baillie (attended 1908-1909) became a famous singer, especially of oratorio.

Angela Brazil (attended 1877-1880) was a writer of girls' school stories. Kathleen Hale (attended 1913-1917) became an author and illustrator of Orlando the Cat books. Another writer was Mollie Greenhalgh (attended 1930-1934), the author of numerous novels and a scriptwriter for such television productions as Upstairs, Downstairs. Television presenter and author, Judy Finnigan, (attended 1959-1966) is another well-known former pupil.

*Top: Manchester High School for Girls, 1913. **Above left:** Pictured in the 1890s are Christabel, Sylvia and Adela Pankhurst, daughters of Emmeline Pankhurst, leader of the British suffragette movement. **Right:** The school tennis team of 1899.*

Clara Freeman (née Jones) (attended 1964-1968) became the first woman executive of Marks & Spencer in 1996 whilst Merlyn Lowther (attended 1965-1972) became the first woman Chief Cashier of the Bank of England in 1999.

Elsewhere, the professions have been well represented. Carrie Morrison (attended 1904-1907) became the first Englishwoman to qualify as a solicitor in 1922. Edith Hesling (attended 1913-1917) became England's first female county court judge. In more recent times, Ann Alexander (attended 1963-1972) was the lawyer who represented the families of the patients who were murdered by Dr Harold Shipman.

In academia, biologist Philippa Esdaile (attended 1896-1907) was one of the first women lecturers at London University. In 1929, Marjorie Jordan (attended 1889-1890) became one of first women students at The Royal Veterinary College, London. Yvonne Barton (attended 1968-1975) became the first female student at Trinity College, Cambridge.

In politics, in 1997 Louise Ellman (attended 1957-1964) became MP for the Liverpool Riverside constituency.

Premises

The school's first premises were two converted terraced houses on Oxford Road on the site of the present Manchester University Medical School. This was chosen because it was in the centre of the intellectual quarter of Manchester; the university was across the road and the Schiller Institute and the former home of the novelist Elizabeth Gaskell were nearby. A Preparatory School was opened in 1876 in another converted house on Oxford Road.

The school opened in 1874 with three teachers and 62 pupils. By 1880, the school had 35 teachers and over 300 pupils. A new school was built on Dover Street, off Oxford Road. This building is now owned by Manchester University. It was the school's home until expanding numbers necessitated yet another move.

In 1940, a new school was opened on Grangethorpe Road, beside Platt Fields. The site had previously been occupied by the Grangethorpe Hospital, originally built for men wounded in the First World War. The spacious 11 acres at Grangethorpe gave room for expansion and the school's premises have been steadily growing ever since with the addition of a new library, a new dining room, a Music House, a swimming pool, a Sixth Form Centre and, most recently, extra accommodation for the Preparatory Department.

Curriculum

The school's curriculum has always been liberal and forward-looking. The first Mathematics teacher was Sarah Woodhead, one of the UK's first women graduates. Within a few years Botany had developed into Biology, Chemistry and Physics. French was traditionally taught in girls' schools, but at Manchester High there were also lessons in German, Spanish, Latin and Greek. Even Domestic Science, the archetypal female subject, included Mathematics and Science, with theoretical as well as practical knowledge. As opportunities for clerical work for women increased at the beginning of the 20th century, a secretarial course was introduced, but this also had an academic bias and included French and German so that girls could become multi-lingual secretaries.

The curriculum has adapted to changing times. Russian was taught from the First World War because the Headmistress thought that girls should learn the language of one of the country's allies.

Top left: *A senior student examining a slide under a microscope in the 1900s.* ***Above:*** *A physical education class in 1905.* ***Below:*** *Girls in the chemistry laboratory, 1905.*

The first cohort of girls included the daughters of a cotton spinner, a warehouseman, an ironmonger, a commercial traveller, a manufacturer and a doctor as well as the science teacher at The Manchester Grammar School, the Registrar at Manchester University and Manchester's Chief Medical Officer of Health.

Some of the girls' names reflect their diverse national origins which have also been typical of Manchester's mixed population. Before the first World War among the girls named Smith, Jones and Brown there were Bauerkellers,

As early as 1957 a member of staff attended a course on computers. Nuclear physics was introduced in the 1960s. The curriculum now includes Mandarin, and Sixth Formers have the option to take the International Baccalaureate Diploma or A Levels.

Pupils: social and cultural backgrounds

The pupils have reflected the ever-changing social and ethnic composition of Manchester.

Budenbergs and Buschmanns whose families had come from Germany in the mid-19th century to set up in business in Manchester. There were Cohens, Marks and Goldstones from Manchester's Jewish community. Guessarians, Kamberians and Odabashians came from Armenian families. The Asian and Chinese communities in Manchester are now represented by girls with family names such as Ali, Choudhri, Chan, Wan and Shibahara.

Manchester University

For the first 65 years of its existence, Manchester High was across the road from Manchester University. Manchester High's former pupils were soon among Manchester University's first Arts, Science and Medical undergraduates and graduates. Rooms in the school's premises at Dover Street were used for teaching women students.

Top left: *Girls taking parcels of clothes they had made to the people in need at the beginning of the First World War.* **Above:** *A Biology lesson in the 1920s.* **Left:** *Founders' Day in the Whitworth Hall of Manchester University, 1934.*

One of MHSG's staff, Annie Ellis, was one of Ernest Rutherford's research students at Manchester University in his work on splitting the atom.

In 1907, the British Federation of University Women, the first British organisation of women graduates, was founded at Manchester High; most of its founder members were from the school and its first President was the Headmistress.

Manchester

Manchester High School has reflected its times and its environment both in Manchester and beyond. Margaret Ashton, Manchester's first female councillor was a governor of the school. Manchester Corporation was represented by one of its councillors on the school's governing body.

In the 1890s, members of the Golden Rule Society made clothes for those in need, visited old people in their homes and visited hospitals and work houses.

During the First World War pupils made clothes, bandages and respirators. Old Girls took on the jobs in banks and offices of men who were fighting at the front. Some did factory work including making munitions. One of the staff joined a Quaker group in France to help with relief work. She later went to Warsaw and died of typhoid there. An Old Girl who had qualified as a doctor went to Serbia to work in a field hospital. Groups of Belgian refugees came to Manchester and Manchester High girls acted as translators to those with limited English. One Belgian refugee became a teacher at the school and some refugee children became pupils. After the War, Broughton House in Salford became a home for disabled servicemen. Manchester High had a particular connection with the home for 60 years; girls visited the residents there each week taking gifts and making friends with them.

The school struggled during the Depression of the inter-war years. There were difficulties getting enough coal and coke during the 1926 General Strike and girls arrived very late because of the transport strike. One teacher, however, rode to school on her horse; it was 'stabled' in the school playground and the Headmistress sent out for some hay to feed it.

*Above: A Chemistry lesson in the 1930s. **Below:** Girls perfecting their service swing during a tennis lesson in 1937.*

Manchester High shared the troubles and the challenges of the Second World War. In 1939, hundreds of girls joined the thousands of other children who were evacuated to escape the dangers of enemy bombing. The girls walked in a long crocodile from Dover Street to London Road station (now Piccadilly station) led by the Headmistress to catch trains to safer locations in south Manchester and Cheshire.

In September 1940, the school's brand new premises were opened at Grangethorpe Road in Rusholme. During the Christmas holidays that year the new premises were destroyed in the Manchester blitz. Staff, girls and their parents helped by the staff and boys of The Manchester Grammar School, searched through the rubble for anything which could be salvaged. Immediately arrangements for new premises were made and without losing one day of lessons the school resumed its life scattered in various premises including Cheadle Hulme School, Withington Girls' School and even a room over a clothing shop in Didsbury.

As in the First World War, so in the Second, Manchester High opened its doors to refugees. Jewish girls from Germany joined the school. Those without families were taken in by the parents of existing pupils or were adopted by Manchester's Jewish community. One of the German Jewish refugees became Manchester High's Head Girl and after the war she returned to Germany to work with other young people on reconstruction and relief work.

The school at Grangethorpe Road was rebuilt in the late 1940s and gradually different year groups returned, but it would be the 1970s before there was enough accommodation to bring the Preparatory Department back from its exile in Didsbury.

As Manchester's immigrant population grew, sixth formers joined a scheme in which they visited Asian women in Rusholme to help them improve their English. The wider community was also helped by the school's branch of the Manchester Youth and Community Service whose activities included home decorating and entertaining people in residential care with a road show.

Above and below: Before and after the devastation of the Manchester blitz.

forward-looking and keen to embrace new educational developments.

Students come from a wide social and cultural mix. A means-tested bursary scheme is available to ensure that bright girls from families who might not otherwise be able to afford to send their daughters to MHSG, can benefit from the excellent opportunities at the school.

MHSG aims to enable girls to discover their talents, to be inspired to learn, and to form clear personal values. Teachers encourage the girls to aim high and to work hard to fulfill their hopes and ambitions. MHSG wants its students to be the best they can be – academically and in their wider education, whether that involves their contribution to Sport, Music and Drama or to any one of the broad range of opportunities offered to them.

Politics

Manchester High School's most famous alumni were the Pankhurst sisters who were pupils in the 1890s. The school had a political conscience, however, from its very beginnings. In about 1876, over 40 years before most women were given the vote, the school held a mock election. A Reform Society was set up in the 1880s in which girls defended the right of women not only to vote, but also to become MPs. On 5 July, 1913, the Headmistress and some of the teaching staff even took part in a suffrage march from Manchester to Stockport. Surprisingly, not all women were in favour: the Headmistress recorded that "Crowds watched us, sometimes with hootings, but as we came into Stockport there were showers of stones, fortunately small, from a crowd of women."

Between the wars the school had a very active League of Nations Union in which girls debated the international issues of the day, from refugee work to the crises in North Africa and Manchuria. The tradition of engagement continues today. Now there is a Model United Nations group and an Amnesty International group.

MHSG Today

The school emblem, the ivy leaf, was chosen over a century ago to reflect steadfastness, perseverance and loyalty, for all of which the school is still recognised today.

MHSG offers a seamless education from age 4 to 18 with extensive experience of supporting and encouraging girls, as well as helping them to achieve their best in everything they do. All members of the school community have a strong sense of tradition, but the school is also

Students leave MHSG as well-educated young women, with highly-developed interpersonal skills and a broad range of interests. They are confident in their own worth, prepared for an independent life, and capable of making a positive contribution to the global society. It is from this cornerstone that they go on to pursue varied and fulfilling careers.

Top left: A bird's eye view of MHSG in the 1990s. Left: The school emblem. Above: Double Olympic gold medal winner Dame Kelly Holmes joins the girls' games lesson during her visit to the school in 2007.

Procter & Gamble
An Olympian Company

When the International Olympic Committee was seeking sponsorship for the 2012 Olympic games in London, Procter & Gamble (P&G) was quick to step up to the mark. And not only for 2012, the company also committed itself to global sponsorship of the Olympic movement for a whole decade.

Like the Olympic movement, Procter & Gamble too is a worldwide phenomenon. The breadth of the company's portfolio, which includes 22 brands alone generating $1 billion or more in annual sales, and the depth of P&G's reach to four billion customers worldwide, makes for a far-reaching Olympic partnership. Some of company's most iconic brands participating in the partnership include Pampers, Ariel, Always, Crest, Pantene and Olay.

Procter & Gamble has had a production facility near Manchester for more than 75 years. But the history of the company goes back much further.

An English candle-maker, William Procter, and an Irish soap-maker, James Gamble, moved to the USA to seek their fortune. Both found themselves living in Cincinnati, Ohio. It was here that they married and became brother in laws. Four years after the wedding in 1837 they formed a partnership which was to become the giant Procter & Gamble company.

In the late 1920s P&G contemplated its first move outside North America. Europe was still getting over the ravages of the Great War and many businesses were going through hard times. Thomas Hedley, a soap-making company based in Newcastle and founded in 1837, was or such organisation - though it was still sufficiently good shape to ensure that Procter & Gamble had to pay a m pounds for the business whose e brands included the famous Fairy a brand it introduced in 1898.

Procter & Gamble took over Thomas Hedley & Co in 1930, though the Hedley name would be retained until 1962.

1931 saw the introduction of Oxydol into the UK market, where it quickly established itself as a washday favourite. The introduction of Lava and Sylvan Flakes washing products caused such heavy demand that new factories were needed. Sylvan Flakes became the pioneers of giant economy packs. New product categories are entered with the introduction of Mirro, 'never scratch' cleanser and Drene, the shampoo of the stars.

Trafford Park in Manchester proved to be ideal. The Trafford Park estates had been the site of Sir Humphrey de Trafford's mansion.

*Top: Founders, William Procter and James Gamble. **Left and below:** Construction of Procter & Gamble's Trafford Park site in 1933.*

Sir Humphrey so disliked seeing merchant ships sailing past his property along the Ship Canal, constructed in 1894, that he sold the 1,200 acre estate - though not before building a ten foot high wall five miles long in attempt to hide the canal from his view.

The estate was sold to a private company for £360,000 and subsequently broken up by lots. Slowly the land nearest to the centre of Manchester became an industrial complex, though the western part of the Park would be undeveloped for many years: it was the site of the Royal Agricultural Show, a golf club, a horse market, stock yards, a polo ground and even, in 1910, an aerodrome. In 1931, ten acres were leased to P&G at 9d a square yard. In 1933 that land was purchased outright.

At the time of its opening in 1934 the Manchester factory would be the world's largest soap and candle factory. The original products of household soap, candles and scouring powder grew and expanded to reflect consumers' increasing and changing demands. New brands were added, new buildings put up and additional land acquired.

Such was the demand for products that Manchester factory doubled in size by 1936.

By July, 1940, Trafford Hall itself had been converted for use as a prisoner of war camp; during the night of 22nd-23rd it was badly damaged by a land mine. Another bomb came through the next door factory roof and landed in a frame of soap two floors below without exploding. Four men - Frank Poole (the works manager) Tom Alexander (who had just been blown 30 feet through the air when the land mine had exploded) George Harris and Tom Evans - coolly pushed the soap frame into the

*Top: The finished factory in 1934. **Above left:** An early view inside the Fairy Snow packaging department. **Below:** Army vehicles outside the factory in during the war years.*

processes ticking over until the all clear sounded. Meanwhile air raid wardens would keep watch on the factory roof.

When Henry Hickson arrived at the factory each morning his job was to go around looking for unexploded bombs and incendiaries. One large piece of shrapnel from a bomb had flown in through a window and embedded itself in the in-tray on the Chief Engineer, Dick Hall-Craggs' desk!

lift and took it out to the canal bank, so saving the factory from heavy damage. The fearless four were later presented with gold mementoes by the Managing Director at a ceremony held in the canteen.

The following night there was another potentially highly dangerous incident: a number of incendiary bombs fell on the roof of the factory's gas holder and another employee, Henry Galgut, climbed up and kicked them off one by one. On the morning of the 24th the main entrance to Trafford park was barricaded off because of the unexploded land mines and bombs lying around.

Trafford Park would be a prime target for the German bombers. When the air raid warning sounded most P&G employees had to go into the air raid shelter under what would become the STU silo unloading area. Only a few key operators would be left in the plant to keep the

Meanwhile, labour shortages were making themselves felt, and although 530 employees were at work staff had to be brought down from Newcastle; able-bodied men were also recruited from the Irish Republic, and for the first time married women were employed to ensure the continued production of 63,000 tons annually of Mirro, Oxydol, Sylvan Flakes and Fairy soap.

In February, 1942, the Government introduced soap rationing. All British manufacturers' packs were now standardised: the four-weekly ration was one 8oz bar of toilet soap or one 12oz packet of soap powder per person (though there were extra rations for children, miners and chimney sweeps).

The Government controlled the manufacture of all soap for the next eight and a half years. What is not widely appreciated is how much soap, and its component element, glycerine, contributed to the war effort. In wartime, supplies of glycerine were of vital importance in the manufacture of explosives for shells and grenades. P&G's process of glycerine recovery was so efficient that other firms sent their lye to London and Manchester for P&G to extract the glycerine. Soap too was very important - it was necessary for the maintenance of hygiene in bomb-damaged areas and in

Top: Procter & Gamble Fairy Soap fleet. **Centre, left and above:** At work in the late 1940s and early 1950s.

the theatres of war all over the world; soap was also used for cooling cutting tools on the lathes which made bullets and shells - and in addition up to 20 tons at a time were used for greasing the slipways each time a ship for the Royal Navy or Merchant marine was launched. The supply of soap and glycerine was so vital to the country's war effort that P&G even manufactured competitors' products at nil profit while their bomb-damaged factories were being rebuilt.

In 1945, a Factory Victory Dance was held in the Longford Hall, Stretford; after almost six years of war the employees could enjoy themselves again. And the work would now be a little easier: that year the first power-driven fork-lift trucks were introduced. Now the heavy loads in the warehouse could be put on pallets and moved by machine instead of muscle power.

Brands now being produced at Manchester included Olivso Bar, Trafford Bar, Cream Suds, Snowhite Flakes, Super Curd Flakes and Scourox. There was, however, still a world-wide shortage of oils and fats, and the soap ration, far from ending after the war, was actually reduced in June, 1946, and finally abolished in September 1950. The Hedley

Chemical Division therefore invented 'Freedom', a detergent washing up powder soon popular with housewives who wanted to double their soap ration.

Dreft was reintroduced in 1947 for use in hard water areas. Extremely popular before the war, Dreft production had ceased in 1940 as some raw materials needed for its manufacture were unobtainable. Because No 1 Tower (the original Oxydol tower) had a stainless steel lining it was now converted at a cost of £33,750 to make Dreft whilst Oxydol production was switched to the smaller No 2 Tower.

Top: This view shows how much the site had expanded by 1961. **Left:** The introduction of computers at Procter & Gamble. **Below left and below:** Production of Flash and Lenor in the 1980s.

produce fatty acid and sweetwater on a continuous basis. The fatty acid was then turned into soap. The new unit, the CSM (Continuous soap-Making Unit), started up in May 1950; at a cost of £200,000 it provided a great boost to productivity and also flexibility as soap brands could be quickly interchanged. That same year a new Hedley product developed in Manchester named 'Tide' was produced in London. Tide caused a sensation, what one newspaper called 'the new washday miracle'. Nor was Tide the only miracle of 1950: soap was de-rationed that September partly as a result of the pressure being taken up by new synthetic detergents. In anticipation everyone worked flat out to have stocks ready to meet the expected surge in demand with a long line of vans and lorries parked nose to tail along Trafford Park Road waiting to be loaded.

Expansion followed; the site of the old Trafford Hall was bought whilst more than half a million pounds was invested in a Tide production tower. The 1950s would see the introduction of many more new household names such as Flash and Fairy Snow.

Another return after the war was the factory buzzer. Many factory hooters could be heard once more sounding over Trafford Park to mark the start of the day's work. Each firm had its own sound varying from the deep-sounding many-toned buzzer at Metro-Vickers to the shrill, tinny notes from small engineering works. The Hedley buzzer was unusual in that it was sounded twice, once at five to eight and again at eight. It often happened that employees sitting in a bus near Carborundum Ltd would hear the first buzzer sound and then the progress of their bus would be stopped by a trainload of wagons crossing the road. The more athletic employees would jump off the bus and race down to clock-in on time, whilst the less athletic sat in the bus knowing that they would be late.

By 1959, the company was producing eight times its initial output and employing 800 people. New brands such as Fairy Liquid, Camay and Synthetic granules were introduced to meet the new demands of consumers. Products such as Lenor and shampoo were moved to Manchester from other P&G sites.

Top left: In the top left of the picture is a new extension for the production of Charmin and Bounty products, 1999. **Above:** The pampers range, produced at Procter & Gamble, Manchester, and Mum's No1 Choice in the UK & Ireland Award label. **Below left and below:** Inside the Pampers factory.

A major step was taken to modernise soap making In the late 1940s. For nearly three years a new structure could be seen taking shape in the tank field just east of the Kettle House. The main part of the equipment was a vertical tube 80 ft long. This structure was the latest method of producing soap - by hydrolysis. At very high temperatures and pressures oil and water reacted to

In 1962, another 23 acres of the park was leased, an event which coincided with an official name change from Hedley & Co Ltd to Procter & Gamble Limited. Over the next 30 years the Manchester site would change its output many times. From soaps, edible oils - margarines and cooking oils - and washing powders to shampoos, conditioners and disposable nappies, reflecting the changing needs of customers and the company's willingness and ability to adapt to changing markets.

A new Paper Module opened in 1991 and 650 more staff were taken on. By the late 1990s the plant would have three modules: Paper, Health and Beauty Care and Distribution. Now P&G would expand once more with a major installation to manufacture Tissue Towel products. By the start of the 21st century the company would be employing some 700 staff and be more efficient than ever before.

which operate with a low-skilled workforce. After massive investment over many years Procter & Gamble and its employees can be proud to have a fast-moving, hi-tech facility with the capacity and capability to support its rapidly growing markets.

Procter & Gamble truly deserves the accolade of 'Olympian'.

Left: Plant Manager (2007-2011) Chris Horner and Jane Thomson (left) welcome the Mayor and Mayorees of the borough of Trafford to Procter & Gamble's 75th Anniversary Open Day. *Top right:* Jane Thomson and some favourite characters at an events day also organised as part of the company's anniversary celebrations. *Above:* Demolition of the original building in 2007. *Below:* Procter & Gamble's Trafford Park site, 2012.

In 2009, the company celebrated 75 years at Trafford Park.

Today, with 135,000 employees worldwide, Procter & Gamble sells around 300 brands to some 4.4 billion consumers in more than 140 countries. Total annual sales exceed $80 billion. The Trafford Park facility is one of more than 100 manufacturing sites. Local soap production has long since ceased, and since 2007 the Manchester site has concentrated exclusively on the production of Pampers nappies. The investment of £175 million in the early years of the 21st century, mainly to update tissue and nappy manufacture, has been matched by the highly capable and technically skilled workforce - the key element which distinguishes Manchester from some other plants

Manchester Arndale
A Shoppers' Paradise

anchester Arndale is the UK's largest inner-city shopping centre. Located right in the heart of the city, it features over 240 shops and has hundreds of high street brands under one roof. There are also numerous restaurants, cafés and fast food outlets located in and around the centre to accommodate hungry shoppers. It is rightly described as the 'jewel in the city's retail crown'.

Manchester's original Arndale Centre was built between 1971 and 1979 by developers, Town & City Properties, the successors to the Arndale Property Trust, with financial backing from the Prudential Assurance Company and Manchester Corporation (City Council). The first phase opened in 1975. The Arndale Property Trust was formed in the early 1950s and took its name from its founders, Yorkshire property developers Arnold Hagenbach and Sam Chippindale. Arndale Property Trust first bought property north of Market Street in 1952.

Manchester Corporation recognised before the end of the Second World War that the area around Market Street was in need of redevelopment. The area was a patchwork of mostly run down Victorian buildings on a 17th and 18th century layout of streets, alleys and courts. Some called it a 'maze of characterful streets'. 'The Seven Stars' on Withy Grove was one of Manchester's oldest pubs, with a license dating back to 1356; it was claimed to be oldest licensed house in Great Britain. Thomas de Quincey, the essayist best known for 'Confessions of an English Opium-Eater', was born in the area on Cross Street in 1785.

In the early 1960s, the area had a vibrant music scene in its many 'coffee beat clubs', which despite being unlicensed, were described in a 1965 a police report as 'dirty, poorly illuminated and being patronised by individuals of exaggerated dress and deportment, commonly known as mods, rockers and beatniks'. However, the passing of The Manchester Corporation Act that same year resulted in most of them being closed down. In the early 1970s the Carnaby Street like maze of small streets was home to second-hand book stalls, trendy clothes and record shops.

Manchester Corporation used compulsory purchase orders to speed up redevelopment adding the land and buildings they owned to those acquired by Arndale Property Trust.

In 1965 the scheme, then costed at £15 million, bounded by Market Street, Corporation Street, Withy Grove and High Street, was intended to be the UK's biggest shopping centre. The boundaries expanded in 1973 onto the site of the former Manchester Guardian offices on the opposite side of Market Street. Boots The Chemist took the whole of that 110,000 sq ft extension.

Arndale Property Trust was acquired by Town & City Properties in April 1968. A public enquiry into the development started on 18 June, 1968; the scheme was to include seven public houses and a 200-bed hotel. The enquiry reported in early November 1969 and the inspector approved the scheme, noting that the region north of Market Street needed redeveloping and wisely observed that it would be sensible to redevelop the shop frontages. Manchester Corporation compulsorily purchased a further eight acres of property in 1970.

The developers demanded a closed-off building with little natural light and rejected a more open, roof-lit design. Manchester Corporation insisted on a bus station, market, car parking, an underground railway station and provision for deck access to subsequent developments. Cannon Street was to be kept open with no shop frontages. Corporation Street and High Street were allowed shop fronts on the returns to Market Street. Market Street, a busy thoroughfare, had shop fronts as pedestrianisation was proposed, though this did not happen until 1981.

Construction started in 1972 and the centre opened in stages. The Arndale Tower and 60 shops opened in September 1976, followed by Knightsbridge Mall (the bridge over Market Street) in May 1977 and the northern mall in October 1977. The market hall, Boots The Chemist and the bridge to the Shambles (over Corporation Street) opened in 1978, as well as the bus station off Cannon Street and anchor stores, followed by Littlewoods and British Home Stores in 1979. On opening, the centre contained 210 shops and over 200 market stalls.

Facing page: Entrances to Manchester Arndale from Exchange Square and Market Street. **Top left:** *Exchange Court showcasing some of the centre's flagship retailers.* **Below and above:** *The Wintergarden mall and its impressive glass roof.*

The cost, estimated at £11.5 million in 1968, rose to £30 million by 1974, forcing the formation of Manchester Mortgage Corporation, a partnership of Town & City, the Prudential Assurance Company and Manchester Corporation. The joint company run by Manchester Corporation raised £5 million on the stock market after the Prudential Assurance Company admitted it could not fully fund the project.

Town & City came close to bankruptcy, forcing it into a reverse takeover of Jeffrey Sterling's Sterling Guarantee Trust in April 1974 and a £25 million rights issue. Costs reached £46 million by 1976, of which £13 million came from the City Council. The final cost was £100 million made up of £11.5 million for land, £44.5 million for the building and £44 million for fitting out. The centre was divided by Market Street and Cannon Street. The part between them was mainly two-storey buildings and contained most of the anchor stores and

access to the office block. Ground-level entrances were at the upper level from High Street and at the lower level from Corporation Street, taking advantage of a slope of about 24 feet (7m). A centrally-placed entrance from Market Street was entered via a mezzanine full-height open space called Hallé Square.

North of Cannon Street, the lower floor was occupied by the bus station, with the upper floor shops and 60 flats, Cromford Court, above them. At the High Street end was a two-floor market area. Cannon Street was bridged by a mall at the Corporation Street end and linked by a tunnel at the High Street end. There was a continuous pathway around the centre but not at a single level. At the High Street end a multi-storey car park was sited above the market centre and Cannon Street. In all there were 1,240 metres of mall. Underneath the centre was a full-circuit, full-height service road, with access from Withy Grove. By taking advantage of the change in height, the architects hoped to solve the problem of persuading shoppers to use the upper shopping area. While the northern part had no anchor stores, the car park and bus station meant that pedestrian traffic passed through the area avoiding quiet spots. The underground railway scheme was abandoned by 1976 and the only deck access was across Corporation Street to another Town & City development in the Shambles.

HRH The Princess Royal officially opened Manchester Arndale in 1979. The previous year, however, The Guardian described the development as 'an awful warning against thinking too big in Britain's cities', and 'so castle-like in its outer strength that any passing medieval army would automatically besiege it rather than shop in it...'.

Top left: The original much-criticised yellow tile-clad 1970s shopping centre. Left and below: How Market Street (left) and the corner of Corporation Street and Withy Grove (below) looked before redevelopment.

The critics' opinion did not mellow with time. The Economist noted in 1996 that it had 'long been regarded as one of Europe's ugliest shopping centres'.

The Financial Times in 1997 called it 'outstandingly ugly', and in 2000 'one of Britain's least-loved buildings'. The main cause of its poor reception was its external appearance. Most of the centre was covered by pre-cast concrete panels faced with mainly yellow ceramic tiles.

The typical life span of a shopping centre is about 10-20 years when the owners may decide whether to do nothing, refurbish or demolish. In the case of the original Arndale Centre, refurbishment began about six years after opening. Artificial lighting and undistinguishable malls, with multiple dead ends and no obvious circular route meant that shoppers were 'bewildered by its maze-like intensity'. Criticisms were addressed in a £500,000 upgrade in which roof lights were inserted to allow in daylight and pot-plants introduced. To improve navigation and to tone down the appearance, the flooring of each area was given a distinct colour scheme, decorative ironwork was installed, a fountain placed at one corner and a double-floor height aviary placed at another. The centre's own radio station, Arndale Radio, was also installed. Hallé Square housed a Foodcourt by day which could also be used as a concert area by night.

Town & City changed its name to Sterling Guarantee Trust in 1983 and in February 1985 merged with the Peninsular and Oriental Steam Navigation Company (universally called P&O), also run by Jeffrey Sterling. P&O decided to refurbish Knightsbridge Mall (the bridge over Market Street) and double the rents. Work took place in 1990-1 and the most visible change was a £9 million Foodcourt (Voyagers) in an area not previously open to the public. The refurbishment was a success and increased the centre's popularity. Other refurbishments followed in 1991-3, despite opposition from traders who objected to changes that might take the centre 'up-market'.

This page: *The aftermath of the June 1996 bombing showing damage to the centre and bridge link on Corporation Street. Pictured above is the famous 1887 Victorian pillar box which was one of the only things to survive unscathed.*

As a shopping centre it was outstandingly successful and became extensively well known. It attracted widespread media attention when Manchester indie band, Northside, filmed 'My Rising Star' video on top of the iconic Arndale Tower in 1990. The centre's bus station became Manchester's busiest, handling 30,000 passengers daily by 1991. By 1996 Manchester Arndale was fully let, raised £20 million a year in rents, and was visited by 750,000 people a week.

However, an event would change the history of Manchester Arndale forever. At 9:20am on Saturday, 15 June, 1996, a van containing a 1,500 kg bomb was parked on Corporation Street between Marks & Spencer and Manchester Arndale. At 9:45am a coded warning from the IRA was received by Granada TV. About 80,000 people were cleared from the area by police and store staff. The bomb exploded at 11:15am. Thankfully, nobody was killed, however over 200 people were injured in the blast. Some 1,200 properties on 43 streets were affected. Marks & Spencer and the adjacent Longridge House were condemned as unsafe and were demolished. Manchester Arndale's frontage on Corporation Street and the bridge link were structurally damaged. The cost was estimated at over £400 million.

However, out of the wreckage arose a new and far better Manchester Arndale - the one we see today.

In the aftermath of the massive damage, the southern half of the centre was extensively repaired, rebuilt and refurbished. The northern half was temporarily patched up, with buses stopping on Cannon Street itself, before eventually being replaced by Shudehill Interchange in January 2006. Marks & Spencer re-opened, linked to the main mall by a glass bridge link. Later the building was split into two independent shops. Half remained a branch of Marks & Spencer while the side facing The Triangle became a branch of Selfridges. As part of the renovation most of the shopping centre's once-reviled tiles were replaced by sandstone and glass cladding. To respond to its new contemporary image the centre was rebranded in 2003 as Manchester Arndale.

In Autumn 2003, at the final stage of rebuilding, all the half of the centre north of Cannon Street was closed and demolished. Over the next three years the northern half of the centre was completely rebuilt and extended. The first phase of the northern extension, known as Exchange Court, opened on 20 October, 2005. This was followed by the second phase, known as New Cannon Street, which opened on 6 April, 2006. Stores in this phase included a new flagship branch of Topshop and Topman.

On 7 September, 2006, the third and final phase of the northern extension opened. The new Wintergarden mall featured stores such as a new HMV, a Waterstones bookshop and a new single-level unit for the Manchester Arndale Market. The completed mall provides a link from Exchange Square and The Triangle to the Northern Quarter and from Market Street to The Printworks. The southern half of the centre was refurbished; Hallé Square was modernised, including new skylights.

Top left: *Demolition of the old shopping centre in 2003.*
Left: *A rooftop view of the reconstruction in June 2004.*
Above: *The frontage of the new Next store begins to take shape, 2004.*

Back in 2004, Manchester Arndale was delighted to invite the world-famous humorist and travel writer Bill Bryson to perform the opening ceremony at its refurbished southern section. The choice of Bill Bryson was particularly apt: ten years earlier the author, with his trademark wit, had memorably described Manchester Arndale as 'the world's largest gents' lavatory' on account of its proliferation of yellow tiles.

When re-opening the southern section, he was delighted to see what had been achieved in making the centre's outside match the glories of its inside.

Today, Manchester Arndale is jointly owned by Prudential Assurance Company Ltd and Capital Shopping Centres. The centre has a retail floorspace of just under 1.5 million sq ft making it the UK's largest inner-city shopping centre with over 40 million 'footfalls' each year.

Recent research (FSP Shopper Survey March 2011) found that 49% of its shoppers are active promoters of Manchester Arndale and would recommend shopping there to a friend. This is well above the average for shopping centres and one of the highest recorded by FSP.

As its marketing strapline states, 'the centre of your city', Manchester Arndale is now an iconic shopping destination and as Manchester Evening News commented: 'Once it was a blot on the landscape, now it's a shoppers' paradise!'

Above: *Manchester Arndale houses Next's largest retail store in the UK and Ireland with a total floor space of 80,000 sq ft.* *Left:* *A view over New Cannon Street with its new improved overhead glass ceiling.* *Below:* *Updated in 2011, the bridge link joining the centre to Marks & Spencer and Selfridges across Corporation Street.*

ITAC Limited
Formulating Success

With over a century of successful formulation development and manufacturing experience the adhesives and coating company ITAC Limited, is today at the forefront of a technical revolution. The company's expanded laboratory provides first class facilities for the development of a technically advanced range of industry specific adhesives and coatings.

Based at Bankfield Mills, Radcliffe, near Manchester, ITAC owes its early impetus to a remarkable man called John Marcus, and just as much to his wife Miriam, who was quite a character.

The business that her husband had started up was not exactly the kind of thing the average young lady would have wanted to get involved with at the turn of the century. Other women might have been content to play the piano in the drawing room or to take afternoon tea with a neighbour. But John's wife was a woman of a different calibre. She had a thread of steel running through her, and she was totally behind her man. If that meant getting her hands dirty then so be it.

It was in 1902 that John Markus had found a niche for his particular talents. He discovered that tyre scrapings, when dissolved in solvent made an excellent rubber adhesive, and when painted onto the outside textile carcass of the tyre, formed an ideal priming coat on which the tyre tread could be bonded.

Working from an attic in premises in Cheetham Hill, John set up the India Rubber & Tyre Company. It was Miriam, however, who had the job of walking down Deansgate to Knott Mill to collect the tyres for processing. Over her shoulder the tyres would go, and the valiant young woman would trudge back to the house bowed down with her heavy burden. After the tyres had been treated she would carry them all the way back again.

One of John Markus's original formulation notebooks still survives today, and a page from the old notebook reads like a book of magic spells: "a few ounces of antimony, a pound or two of sulphur, a gallon or so of naphtha; add whitening, zinc oxide, magnesia, litharge and a touch of bag black for colour", and there you have it - only without the eye of a newt and toe of a frog.

Despite the march of polymer science, a number of the ingredients used by the company for today's rubber solutions have remained the same through the years, though naturally the equipment and the technology has kept pace with the times.

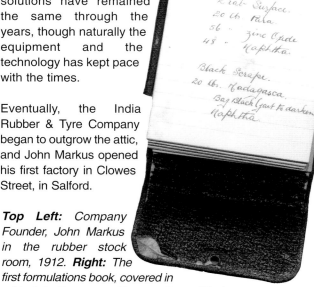

Eventually, the India Rubber & Tyre Company began to outgrow the attic, and John Markus opened his first factory in Clowes Street, in Salford.

Top Left: Company Founder, John Markus in the rubber stock room, 1912. **Right:** The first formulations book, covered in a black leather case with a small pencil hole.

Big mixing vats formed the largest part of the firm's original equipment, and as the company expanded the equipment and the materials became more complex.

Changes in tyre manufacturing techniques meant that the company had to find a new outlet for its products. At that time in the city of Manchester there was a thriving industry developing in the manufacture of the traditional rubber proofed raincoats. The process of making waterproof fabric from rubber proofed textile had been invented by Charles Macintosh some 90 years earlier, and basing his factory in Manchester had spawned over 50 manufacturers of rubber proofed garments.

To be fully waterproof, the seams of the coats or capes had to be sealed and this was done by "schmearing a varnish" onto a tape made from the same waterproof fabric by finger, and then bonding this tape to the underside of the seam. This was an area the India Rubber & Tyre Company was at home in, so it seized the opportunity. The company was not alone in the field however.

There were about half a dozen such companies which met annually to agree prices within the Manchester area. At the time this was, of course, totally legal.

The India Rubber and Tyre Company was a family firm in the true sense of the word, and its women were determined to play a key role. In time John's daughter, Mrs. Irene Ross, joined the firm in 1929 following her father's death, despite having never worked in a factory before. Her daughter Anne would follow her. When war broke out in 1939, it was Irene Ross who continued in her father's footsteps.

The general shortage of materials during the war became a real headache to the firm. One of the company's customers however, gave the timely help that it needed by managing to secure for the company a contract to provide the army with ground sheets. The ongoing order proved to be a real break, and the contract continued to the end of the war and beyond.

After Mr. Alan Armitt joined the company in 1954, it experienced a further stage in its development. He introduced polyurethane technology to the firm. Polyurethane came into the factory in the form of granules. It was put into solution with other additives and then sold to the textile coating industry. The solution was not for the seams alone, but this time to give the textile itself a waterproof finish.

The company now made a second move, to premises in Blackburn Street, in Salford. It was there that the India Rubber & Tyre Company made a more defined move towards expansion. The acquisition of an adhesive manufacturing business in 1970 led to a change of name to India Rubber & Tyre Adhesives Co Ltd, which was shortened to 'ITAC' in 1972 when the company moved to its current site in Radcliffe, Manchester.

Alan Armitt now introduced a marketing strategy, which realised the full potential of ITAC's mixing equipment, and began to manufacture adhesives in addition to coating solutions.

Top Left: *Irene Esther Ross who took over from her father when he died in 1928, having never worked at the factory before.* ***Left:*** *The late Alan Armitt, former chairman and managing director.*

Alan's day-to-day input, however, was sadly missed. Determined to go forward, Paul Armitt placed a great emphasis on bringing the company up-to-date, and during the 1990s a new computer system was installed, the factory and offices were refurbished and the company image was given a face-lift. Since then Itac has concentrated on building up a team of skilled staff with the determination and expertise to drive the company forward.

In 1998, ITAC acquired the European quality standard BS EN ISO 9001: 2008 and a short time later the company achieved the prestigious Investors in People award. Both of which would provide further opportunities for growth and expansion while continuing to support their existing markets. Building on the solid foundation of their many years of experience and the expertise of its workforce, ITAC began actively pursuing opportunities for acquisitions as well as organic growth. The overall plan was to grow and develop the company and to go forward into the new millennium supplying an extended range of clients with the same high standard of service that had always been provided.

Two acquisitions were soon made: Crispin Adhesives, and Borden Speciality Water Based Adhesive division.

One dreadful March day, in 1988, however, fire swept through the plant, completely destroying much of its equipment and materials. Bloodied but unbowed, ITAC turned the disaster around, and when repairs and renovations got underway the company took the opportunity to re- equip the plant with the latest mixing plant and machinery.

The early 1990s proved to be a difficult time. There were internal problems to deal with in addition to the necessity of facing the general recession. In September 1991, a stroke brought Alan Armitt's involvement with the company to an untimely end, and his son Paul Armitt took over the reins of the company a few months later, in January 1992.

Despite such acquisitions the poor economic climate leading up to 2005 meant ITAC was forced to reduce costs, in order to remain commercially viable. In 2005, it put in place a restructuring plan, which reviewed its pricing structure and reduced the workforce.

This timely action successfully returned ITAC to profitability.

Paul Armitt was determined to ensure that this family business should grow, so profits were reinvested into the company. The aim during those difficult times was to continually look at ways in which ITAC could demonstrate to customers that it could come up with

Top Left: *Burnt out factory after the fire, 1988.*
Left: *Inspecting product during manufacture.*

innovative ways in which to offer better value for money by doing the basic things better, not least in packaging, waste disposal, and passing on the cost advantages of bulk buying.

The company took on an additional management resource in the form of Tony Cross who enhanced strategic planning also taking responsibility for purchasing. At this time ITAC realized it needed to change the way it got it's marketing message across. The company had a long-term relationship with marketing design firm, Myers & Myers Associates. The

Aiming to go a stage further, ITAC has introduced a Statistical Process Control system into its production process that allows customers to access – password protected quality control data on line, through the company's website. This information is given in both tabulated and graphical form providing an 'at a glance' facility to analyse historical data for the last 6 months or 30 batches.

Above: Main manufacturing plant Left: Product sample in the laboratory Below: ICB container being filled

South Manchester consultants, now became more involved with ITAC, creating an integrated marketing campaign including rebranding and the development of a new website. The ITS – intelligent technical solutions initiative was launched. This promoted ITAC's knowledge base and formulation skills. In conjunction with the marketing, further investment took place when the laboratory team was strengthened, with the appointment of Elizabeth Henderson as Product Development Manager.

Traditionally, ITAC had taken a reactive position, waiting for or encouraging customers to present opportunities to which it could respond. Now ITAC began to look for strategic partners who had leading edge technologies that would support the advanced adhesive and coating solutions that Itac wanted to develop. In this way the company provides added value solutions to its customers and solves problems before they arise. Recent successes can be seen in their Switchable adhesives and ITS Reveal technology.

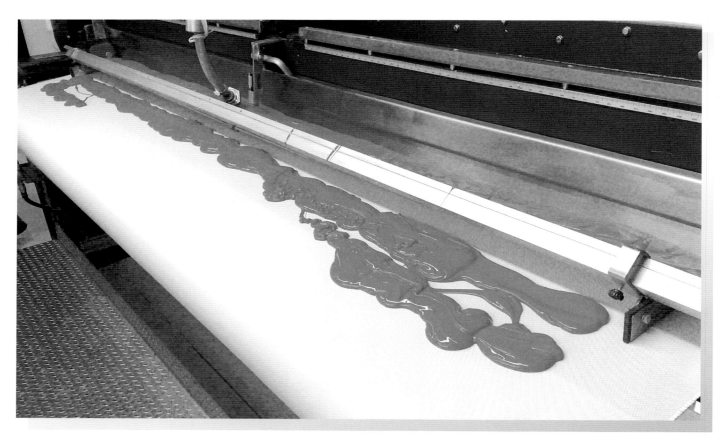

This initiative has helped to optimise customers' specific production processes demonstrating consistency of quality. ITAC believes that it is the only business within its sector able to offer this facility.

Despite continued recent global economic instability, ITAC has still been able to grow the business. In the financial year ending 2011, it posted a growth of 48% on the previous year, returning a top line sales value of just over £4m - a tremendous testament to the effort of all who worked towards this success.

In August 2011, ITAC acquired Texas Coatings and Developments of Rawtenstall and that business has now been successfully incorporated into ITAC.

2012 will see a complete refurbishment of ITAC's reception area and a refit of its bulk solvent distribution facility, demonstrating the Company's further commitment to the future, its employees, customers and suppliers. Almost half the company's sales today are involved in supplying technical textile coatings. Once an ITAC coating solution is applied to a fabric it dries to a tack free film, rendering the

Top: ITAC coating being machine applied to a substrate. *Left:* Processing natural rubber *Above:* ITAC brand - ITS Reveal.

textile waterproof, fire retardant or resistant to chemicals. Alternatively, the coating could be heat reactivatable or pressure sensitive as is required by their graphics or surgical dressing customers.

Today's rapid pace of change in the manufacturing industry demands a dedication to research into new methods, machinery and materials. Committed to providing the bespoke manufacturing service that many of its customers' demand, ITAC has developed the ability to interpret precisely customers' requirements. The technical team develop products that add value to the end product and complement their customers' own method of manufacture.

ITAC is proud of its products but it is equally proud of its committed technical and sales support, the high quality of its service and its competitive prices.

From its humble beginning in an attic room in Cheetham Hill, ITAC has become an international player. ITAC adhesives and coatings are doing an important job in products across the globe with exports forming around twenty percent of turnover. The company is sensitive and responsive to the needs of its markets, which include Graphics, Textiles and Construction plus many others. ITAC is confident about the future, it is in a strong financial position with the right systems, equipment and team of people in place. The family business is now set for further planned expansion and growth.

Above: Formulating in the ITAC laboratory. *Below:* A new ITAC truck

Elcometer Ltd - The Measure Of Precision

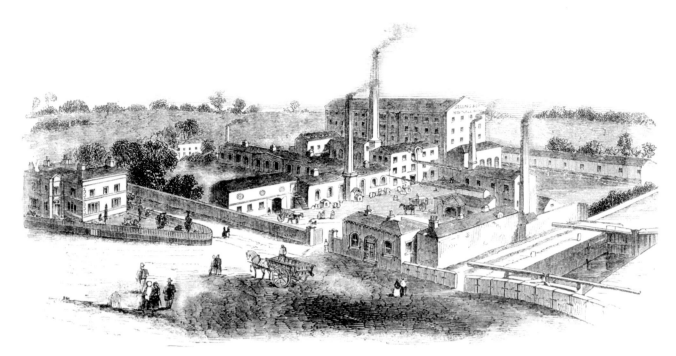

Based in Edge Lane, Manchester, but with offices in the USA, Singapore, Japan, France, Belgium, the Netherlands and Germany, Elcometer Limited is a truly international business. It is also a family firm.

Today, Elcometer is an industry leader in coating and concrete inspection equipment, rebar and industrial metal detection, and ultrasonic thickness and flaw detection equipment. Now employing some 200 staff around the world, the company's products measure a wide range of parameters including coating thickness, climate monitoring, porosity and adhesion as well as a wide range of physical test parameters required for the formulation of coatings.

Soap and starch. Humble products they may be, but these two basic commodities formed the unlikely starting place for what was to become a multi million pound international inspection instruments company.

It was back in the 1830s that Barratt Carrington Sellars founded a business manufacturing starch and soap; since then seven generations of the family have been involved in the business. Trading as Sellars & Co Starch & Soap Manufacturers, Barratt Sellars' first premises were a complex of buildings next to the canal in the Monsall works, Newton Heath. Five tall chimneys huffed and puffed above the factory while in the busy yard below delivery

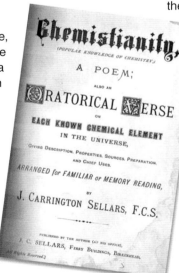

carts and wagons were loaded and unloaded and, pulled by the firm's patient horses, went out on their various journeys.

Within twenty years the company had become the East Lancashire Chemical Co, and during the 1880s a move was made to Edge Lane, in Droylsden. Through expansion, a second facility was added in the 1890s which also took the company to Fairfield Road, also in Droylsden.

The new premises gave the firm the opportunity to expand its range of products, and it began to make cement as well as soap. For a hundred years or so the factory's main products remained the same. One of the company's mainstay products was the industrial soap that it manufactured for use in the textile industry. The firm also made ELCO washing soda and colbit, a bitumen emulsion which was used for road building and tennis courts.

Colbit was made at the factory until the 1980s. Production of cement ceased at the beginning of the Second World War. During this period things progressed as smoothly as

Top: *The original Sellars & Co Soap Manufactory in Newton Heath, Manchester.*
Left: *The cover of a poem book for each known chemical element produced by J. Carrington Sellars.*

It was in 1956 that the company moved into the field of electronic instrumentation. It developed its first transistor instruments in 1960, but sadly John Carrington Sellars died two years later at the comparatively young age of 57. He would have been thrilled to have been there when, in the mid-1970s, the company were the first in the world to use micro processors in a coating thickness gauge.

Peter and Ian Sellars took over the business, and in 1962 Ian renamed the instruments side of the business Elcometer Instruments Ltd. The company's first export order had been to Australia in September 1948. Today, over ninety percent of products are exported around the world, and in 1978 the company won the Queen's Award for Exports

Ian Carrington Sellars took 100% ownership of the Company in 1983. The following year the Elcometer 256, the world's first coating thickness gauge with statistics, was launched.

could be expected for the firm during wartime, and it even survived a bomb that was dropped on the Fairfield Road works.

After the war John Carrington Sellars, who had taken over the reins of the business, realised with real foresight that the textile industry was not going to survive for very much longer. The knock-on effect of that would be a falling off in demand for the firm's industrial soap. It was a chance meeting in a radio shop that provided John Sellars with the alternative product that he knew the company would need in the future. In the shop he chatted with Jim Hartland, who told him about an idea he had for a product he later called the 'Elcometer®', which was an instrument for measuring coatings on steel substrates.

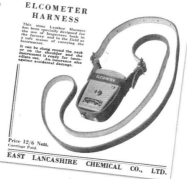

John Sellars instinctively recognised the potential of the instrument, and without hesitation he offered Hartland a job, developed the idea and went into production.

The original Elcometer was essentially a horseshoe magnet with a compass and a spring. The first jewelled bearings for the pivot were bought cheaply as war surplus. The die to mould the case cost £100; it was a lot of money then and John worried that the investment might not pay off. In fact the die would need to be replaced three times after John's original estimate of sales in the hundreds rose to thousands.

The first of the instruments sold for ten guineas (£10.50). When asked why a chemical company would make measuring equipment, John Sellars would come back with the comment that "ICI make zip fasteners - so why not?"

Meanwhile, the company premises continued to grow with eight extensions being built over the years, culminating in 1986 in the building of a purpose-built production facility opened by H.R.H. The Duke of Kent. The original shop floor became the new R&D facility.

Another accolade soon followed with Elcometer gaining the Queen's Award for Technology in 1990.

Top left: *Mr Ian Sellars, 1980.* ***Left:*** *Early advertising for the 'Elcometer'* *Inspector Harness.* ***Below:*** *Elcometer's 50th Anniversary.* *H.R.H. The Duke of Kent with Mr Ian Sellars.*

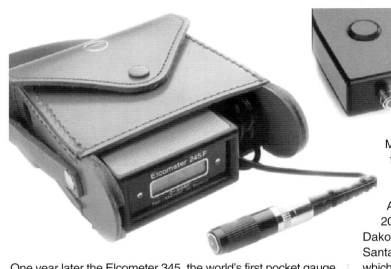

same site, doubling the factory space and adding new production, office and training facilities, totalling 5,110m² (55,000 sq.ft.)

Three months later the company launched the Elcometer 456 Mk 3, the world's first coating thickness gauge with Bluetooth® communications.

Michael Sellars took over the company in April 2008 following the sudden death of his father. Shortly thereafter the company was re-named Elcometer Limited.

Another acquisition came in January 2011, when Elcometer purchased Dakota Ultrasonics Incorporated of Santa Cruz, California, a company which designs and manufactures a comprehensive range of ultrasonic NDT thickness gauges and flaw detectors.

One year later the Elcometer 345, the world's first pocket gauge with statistics and memory, was launched.

In 1995, Michael Carrington Sellars, Ian's son, joined the family business. It wasn't a new experience for him, however, as he had spent most holidays in his youth working at Elcometer.

H.R.H. The Duke of Kent returned to Elcometer in 1997 to help celebrate the firm's 50th anniversary celebration. His Royal Highness was becoming a familiar figure at Elcometer!

More new products soon followed with Elcometer launching its Elcometer 456 in 2000, the world's first digital coating thickness gauge with graphic screen and menu driven softkeys.

In March 2011, exactly 10 years after the launch of the best-selling Elcometer 456 digital coating thickness gauge, Elcometer launched the next generation of Elcometer 456 gauges with colour screen, accelerometer, alpha-numeric memory and remote user gauge upgrades.

In 2003 Elcometer acquired Braive Instruments SA, Belgium, and its French subsidiary, Braive France Sarl – both leading manufacturers of physical test equipment to the paint and powder industry. The two companies became part of the Elcometer worldwide business network and are now known as Elcometer SA and Elcometer SÀRL respectively.

By the end of the year Elcometer had opened another new overseas office, in Tokyo, Japan.

That same year Elcometer also purchased the UK's leading manufacturer of concrete inspection equipment, Protovale (Oxford) Limited, adding a range of concrete inspection and industrial metal detection equipment to its product portfolio.

In July, 2007, Elcometer Instruments Limited celebrated its 60th year and opened its new headquarters on the

Top left: Elcometer's 245F which at the time was the world's smallest, solid state coating thickness gauge for paint, electroplating, galvanising and metal coatings. Right: The company's 250 series of the early 1980s. Top right: The Elcometer 255 Hand Held Microprocessor Based Digital Coating Thickness Gauge.

Despite the high value that the company places on innovation, technical prowess and the quality of its products, it's really people that make the difference at Elcometer.

A highly skilled production workforce builds and assembles the majority of key products in the company's own manufacturing facilities. The UK export team has fluency in several languages, including French, German, Spanish and Ukrainian.

The company firmly believes in the philosophy that when its customers come to Elcometer they are buying a commitment to great service and not just the tangible product. This is proven by the large number that come back to Elcometer to purchase inspection equipment, because they appreciate trustworthy advice and straight talking.

From a turnover of £42,000 in 1962, the company developed into today's multi-million-pound company. All the manufacturing is done at their factories in Manchester, Liege (Belgium) or Santa Cruz, California (USA). They market their products through the company's UK head office, together with its sales and service subsidiaries in the USA, France, Belgium, Germany, Singapore and Japan and its comprehensive global network of distributors in over 60 other countries. The main markets are the automotive, marine, oil and gas, paints and construction industries.

Elcometer is committed to staying at the forefront of technology, investing approximately ten percent of its sales in research. Elcometer's plans for the future are quite simple - to carry on much as it has always done, providing clients with instruments at a cost that reflects the company's commitment to a fair price and allows for new research, new developments - and better products.

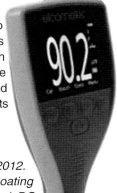

*Top: The Elcometer Head Quarters, 2012. **Above:** An Elcometer Protective Coating Kit. **Left:** The Elcometer 280 Pulsed DC Holiday Detector. **Right:** The Elcometer 456 Integral Gauge, launched in 2011.*

Sykes Seafood - Quality Since 1862

Fish don't have labels. But if they did it's a good bet that they would read 'Supplied by Sykes Seafoods of Manchester'.

Manchester's New Smithfield Market, in Whitworth Street East, Openshaw, opened its doors for business in 1973. The old Smithfield Market which the new building replaced was built in 1822. At its peak, at the start of the 20th century, it was probably the largest market complex in Britain.

Best known, and one of the oldest amongst the many firms operating from the market, is J. Sykes & Sons Ltd, seafood wholesalers and distributors. Today the holding company, Sykes Seafoods Ltd, established in 1996, has two trading subsidiaries: J. Sykes & Sons (Manchester) Ltd and Sefton Meadow Seafoods Ltd - an associated prawn packing factory based north of Liverpool which was acquired by Sykes Seafoods in January 2012.

The business was started by Joseph Sykes, the great grandfather of the present owners Martin and David Sykes. Joe Sykes started trading wet fish and Dutch shrimps from the original Smithfield Market in 1862, with deliveries being made by horse and cart well into the 20th Century.

Until the middle of the Victorian era fresh seafood was available in quantity only at the seaside ports where the fish was landed. Some living fish would be transported inland in barrels by packhorse, their price reflecting the high cost of transport. For the working classes sea-caught fish was preserved by smoking or salting. Kippers, not wet fish, were the order of the day.

Above: To the right can be seen the J. Sykes & Sons premises in the old Smithfield Market. Below: At work inside old Smithfield Market.

Ice and speed would provide the solution to supplying fresh fish to the growing city of Manchester. The speed and relatively low cost of transport would be provided by railways. The Liverpool & Manchester Railway opened in 1830 making it possible for freshly caught fish to reach Manchester within hours of landing.

In the mid-19th century it was realised that the speed of steam ships and railways, combined with the insulating properties of sawdust, could make it economical to harvest ice from lakes in Canada and the waters around the Baltic, and tranship it to warmer climes.

Now butchers, fishmongers, and even the better off home owner, could buy blocks of ice which could be kept for up to a week in zinc-lined insulated boxes.

Within a generation, however, the transportation of lake ice would be rendered unnecessary by the invention in 1876 of the ice machine - the basis of modern refrigeration.

Soon refrigerated trawlers meant that fishing vessels could travel further and return to port less frequently, increasing catch sizes and increasing profits, whilst at the same time pushing down prices.

By the 1930s there was fish for everyone at an affordable price. No wonder fish and chips became Britain's national dish.

Following the Second World War the business expanded greatly when the current owners' father, Bill Sykes, looked to the Continent for fish supplies.

Ronald 'Bill' Sykes died in 1996, having worked in the firm until the previous year, by which time he was 75 years old. He had joined the family business in 1935 at the age of 15. At that time his father, William, and his uncles, Arthur and Charlie, were running the firm. By 1938, when Bill took over at the tender age of 18, it had become one of the largest wholesalers on the market. Bill Sykes would be the driving force behind the business, taking it from local to national, and even international prominence.

The fact that there is still a viable fish market in Manchester is very largely due to Bill Sykes. During the 1950s a delivery service was started primarily delivering to fish fryers within a 10-mile radius of Manchester. Bill Sykes was soon moving 1,000 boxes of plaice and 1,000 of hake every week. The firm worked on a profit margin of two shillings (10p) per four stone box of Danish plaice in the 1960s, selling at around 30 shillings (£1.50) per stone.

Chartered accountant Martin Sykes joined the business in 1965 and his brother, fellow accountant David, joined five years later. By 1972 Sykes' was the biggest importer in England of Danish fish, particularly plaice, and later of cod and haddock fillets. The

Above: A aerial view of the site in 1973. **Left:** *Bill Sykes, the driving force behind the business for six decades.* **Below:** *Present owners Martin Sykes (left) and David Sykes*

Today, J. Sykes & Sons imports seafood from all over the world for onward distribution; the Wholesale Division handles full and mixed pallet orders for frozen fish and prawns all over the UK. The Fish Fryers Division supplies fish and chip shops in the North West of England with fresh and frozen fish, burgers, sausages, pies, etc, and full pallets of shatterpack cod and haddock nationally.

The company's Market Division occupies some 25% of Manchester's Smithfield Market Fish Building selling mainly frozen and smoked fish.

company's big break came in 1970 when Bill Sykes was asked to supply MacFisheries depots. By the late 1970s MacFisheries had over 500 shops – and a large proportion of these were served by Sykes.

The company relocated in 1974 to the new market outside the city centre to take advantage of the growing trade in frozen seafood.

In the old market the firm had no fewer than 17 stalls, but they were spread out in inconvenient locations. In moving to the new market Bill Sykes had ensured that all the Sykes' stalls were together. In 1973, always thinking ahead, Bill had also bought an acre of land adjacent to the market on which was built the first 250-pallet cold store. This was extended to 500 pallets in 1990 and then doubled again to 1,000 pallets in 2000. In recent years, cold storage and the national distribution operation has increased substantially, with on-site storage capacity increased 2½ times, up from 1,000 pallets to 2,500.

Expansion, however, has not taken place without serious setbacks. In the late 1970s their largest customer, MacFisheries, closed and half of Sykes' sales were gone. That became the trigger for the company to develop the catering side of the business. The change in direction coincided with the move to the new market.

The Wholesale Division of J. Sykes & Sons supplies full and mixed pallet quantities of frozen seafood to buying groups and individual companies, such as wholesalers, food service distributors, sandwich manufacturers and fish merchants.

The rest of the Foodservice operation consists of wholesale supply to regional distributors throughout the country who in turn supply restaurants, pubs and other low-cost eating establishments.

*Top: Inside the J. Sykes & Sons premises in 2001. **Below:** From left to right: Robert Sykes, Alexander Sykes (sons of David), Matthew Sykes (son of Martin), David Sykes and Martin Sykes.*

Sykes' policy is to make sure it provides the seafood part of their menu, thereby using their local distribution to the end users in areas where Sykes could not operate effectively.

Daily deliveries of fresh fish start at 4am, straight after the market opens, and fish is waiting for fryers when they arrive at their premises in the morning. With some 61 staff working for Sykes, and annual sales worth £55 million and rising, its seafood business is still rapidly expanding.

The emphasis has been on supplying low-cost catering outlets to meet the now well-established culture throughout the country of the enjoyment of eating out. As a result the company has expanded its direct deliveries to the fish frying trade and runs a fleet of 14 refrigerated, fully equipped modern Mercedes vans.

The company has enjoyed a long and illustrious past. With its long and established history of integrity, quality and service and its long-serving and loyal staff, Sykes Seafoods is looking forward to a prosperous future.

As for J. Sykes & Sons' status as a genuine family firm, that looks set to continue far into the future, with the fifth generation of the family as hooked on fish as their great-great grandfather, the firm's founder, Joseph Sykes.

Top: Sykes New Smithfield House. **Left and Below:** *Early morning loading of two of the company's Mercedes artics.*

Sykes seafood is also closely involved with Manchester City Council. The Council is anxious to re-build the site at Openshaw, starting with their new fish market. Sykes is in a position to finance the project, as well as having drawn up plans both for the building of the new market and demolition of the old market.

This project will give Sykes more room to increase its cold storage capacity as well as making the market far more exciting for customers.

Searchlight - A Brilliant Heritage

Searchlight Electric was started in 1945 by Sidney Hamburger. Born in Salford in 1914, the son of poor Jewish immigrants from Poland, he had recently left the army with the rank of Captain; he was Mayor of Salford in 1968, and was knighted in 1984 for services to the National Health.

Sir Sidney, as he would become, possessed a sharp business brain which, combined with his dynamic personality and strong work ethic, ensured Searchlight's success. It was originally started as a one-man wholesale electrical business, selling small electrical appliances.

A highly respected businessman, Sir Sidney also had a devotion to the less fortunate in society, which manifested itself through his many communal activities.

Perhaps the interest in lighting was genetic; Sidney's father had started a gas mantle business in Manchester soon after he arrived in this country. When Sidney left school he took a course in domestic electrical wiring.

Pre-war Sidney worked as a manager for Marks & Spencer. He wrote them a memo in 1937 with a variety of changes which he thought were needed within their display and organisation. Forty years later he came across his recommendations again and sent them to M & S who wrote a very warm letter back saying it was amazing how many of the ideas that he had suggested all those years ago had been implemented - a clear indication of Sidney's early vision.

Discharged from the army in 1945 with a gratuity of £150.00 Sidney didn't want to go back to M & S. He realised that the ambitions he had of public service could never be met as an

*Left: Founder, Sidney Hamburger. **Top:** Where it all began, the company's first showroom. **Below:** The Searchlight team in the 1960s.*

Sidney was soon joined by a colleague in 1946 whom he had met in the army - Bill Stockton. He was a man with a meticulously organised mind and superb handwriting which would have done credit to any calligrapher. He stayed until his retirement in 1980.

Sidney was also joined by his brother David after he too was demobbed in 1947.

In 1949 they moved to basement premises at 15, Blackfriars Street, off Deansgate, in the centre of Manchester, where a small showroom and warehouse were opened and lighting was first introduced into the range of products - almost all made in the U.K. rather than today, when they are mostly imported. Two of Sidney's sons Herzl and Dov joined the business in 1957 and 1961 respectively.

employee in another company, so he was driven to self-employment.

Sidney opened Searchlight in 1945 in a tiny office in the cellar of number 1B Cooper Street, Salford, where supplies were very limited, and none of the major manufacturers wanted to accept

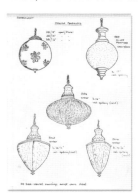

new customers. Their repeated excuse was "We have got to support those who helped us during the war." Nothing annoyed Sidney more than to hear this repetitive response, as though those who had been called up had spent five years relaxing in the Bahamas.

He sold electric kettles, irons, heaters and decorative Christmas lights. Every morning he went out as a salesman with a bag of samples. In the evening he went to the office to collect the goods he had sold; took them home at night to pack, and do the paperwork and invoicing together with his wife Gertrude. The following morning he delivered the goods and repeated the routine.

The policy of the family was that as the sons joined the business, they should do everything in the firm including sweeping up, loading and unloading goods, packing and delivering.

At the age of 17 each son was presented with a Bedford van, told that he was now a traveling salesman and was sent out on the road.

Top left: *The opening of Searchlight's new showroom in 1970. Pictured are Sidney Hamburger (right) and David Hamburger (left) with Ronald Richardson, then Norweb Chairman who opened the new showroom.* ***Centre left:*** *Early sketches of lighting products. Beautifully drawn by Elaine Hamburger, these were used as an early company brochure in 1973.* ***Left:*** *The new impressive showroom, 1970.* ***Above:*** *Dov Hamburger (right) with representatives from Glassexport seated in front of some of the companies dazzling chandeliers.*

Sidney worked incredibly hard in those early days, he often started at 7.00 a.m., finished at 6.00 p.m. and then returned after a hurried evening meal and worked until midnight. The Salford City Reporter often reported that they saw the light in the top office burning long after everybody else had departed. One Saturday afternoon in 1968, only weeks after Sidney had ceased to be Mayor, the premises in Middlewood Street went up in flames. The efforts of the fire fighters were fruitless; Sidney and his sons just had to stand there and watch their future going up in smoke.

This, of course, contributed to the growth of the company as new markets were tackled.

Meanwhile, life for Sidney was extremely difficult because he was already trying to get on the bottom rung of the ladder of social and political activity, with all the conflicting demands on his time.

As Chairman of the Planning Committee on Salford City Council, Sidney had to visit the premises of Dorman Smith, in Middlewood Street, Salford in connection with a planning application. The Managing Director, a Mr Atherton, took Sidney on one side after the Committee members had left and said, "I can't understand a sensible young man like you wasting your time in Local Authority work. You will never get thanks. You really ought to be concentrating on building up your own business." What irony that some years later when Dorman Smith closed its business in Salford, Sidney bought those premises in Middlewood Street and moved there in 1960.

In the following days and weeks, walking through the 'slutch', the burnt out embers and the water-soaked goods, staff really showed a sense of commitment and dedication far beyond anything that was expected of them.

Before the fire the sound of a fire engine had always aroused in Sidney feelings of excitement, anticipation, and an urge to see where they were going.

Top left: *Members of the Hamburger family pictured with former USA President, George Bush Snr. L-R: Morris and Debbie, Sir Sidney and Lady Hamburger, George Bush, Rosemary and Herzl, Elaine and Dov.* **Left:** *Herzl, Morris and Dov Hamburger.* **Top right:** *Searchlight's Showroom in 1982.* **Above:** *A certificate awarded to Searchlight in 2005 for 60 years of continuous growth and customer satisfaction.*

Having stood at the side of his own business, watching it go up in flames, that urge was stifled in minutes.

In November, 1970, after an extensive rebuilding programme the premises were re-opened.

His third son, Morris, joined the firm in 1973.

Once again these premises were outgrown and in 1980 a 195,000 sq ft building was bought in Water Street, Salford.

In 1995, a joint venture factory was opened in Guangdong, China, employing 400 staff.

As the business grew even more a decision was taken to build a state-of-the-art warehouse and showrooms in East Manchester. In 2002 dedicated premises were opened by the Earl and Countess of Wessex on an 8.5 acre site, just 10 minutes from the original site.

The current premises, Sidney House, are at 900 Oldham Road, Manchester. The purpose-built three-storey facility has the largest showrooms in the UK and a fully equipped 95,000 sq ft warehouse. The building was constructed with all the latest warehouse management systems, a computer based electronic picking system - and great attention was paid to safety testing facilities for quality control purposes.

Today, orders are shipped within 24 hours; the £10 million range of stock runs from table lamps at £3.00 to crystal chandeliers at £10,000.

Meanwhile, the continuing family ethos has encouraged loyalty both to and from the staff, many having been with the company for over 30 years.

Company founder, Sir Sidney Hamburger, passed away in 2001. His life's work, however, continues; and not just his business legacy. The charitable work begun by Sir Sidney continues to this day. All the family are involved in a variety of charities throughout the country dedicated to the aged, social welfare and supporting hospitals.

The current Chairman is Herzl Hamburger who sits on the board with Dov, Morris and Daniel, Herzl's son now the third generation of the family. David Joyce is Managing Director and Giselle Lenham is the Commercial Director.

Today, Searchlight believes the future is in export, and is putting a lot of its resources into exhibiting at all the major lighting exhibitions throughout the world, including Hong Kong, Germany and Sweden. The company exports to over 40 countries. A big change from a one man band to now employing 200 staff in the UK.

*Top right: Opening of Sidney House, the new Searchlight state-of-the-art premises in 2002 by the Earl and Countess of Wessex. Their Royal Highnesses are being shown a presentation by Daniel Hamburger. **Left and below:** Interior and exterior views of Searchlight's Sidney House, Oldham Road, Manchester.*

Searchlight is now a key supplier to many of the household names in the UK and is at the forefront of changing lighting trends which now encompass halogen lights and LEDs.

In 2006 an architectural lighting company, Illuma, was acquired. Together both companies employ over 200 people, including a complete design team which prepares unique products for the market.

William Hulme's Grammar School
'Trust, but in Whom Take Care'

In times past many of us stayed on at our local school only until the age of just 14 before leaving for the world of work. Other somewhat younger readers may have attended a 'Secondary Modern' or a brand new Comprehensive school. Still others may have passed their 'eleven-plus' and gone to a Grammar School. And some readers will have attended a school which can trace its history back to the Victorian era, and its roots to events which occurred three centuries ago – Manchester's William Hulme's Grammar School.

William Hulme (1631- 1691) was the founder of the William Hulme Charity. He lived at Hulme Hall (later Broadstone Hall) in Reddish, Stockport. Very little is known about William's life except that he owned two other large properties in the region: one at Withingreave Hall, in Withy Grove, Manchester, and another at Outwood, near Prestwich.

Probably educated in Manchester, William was brought up by an uncle, after his father had died when he was just 11 years old. Opinions differ as to his adult life. Some maintain that he followed a career at Law after attending Brasenose College, in Oxford; others believe that he lived the life of a country gentleman. What we do know with certainty is that he held the position of Justice of the Peace for Kearsley, near Bolton, where his wife Elizabeth had grown up.

The premature and tragic death of his beloved only son was however, to deeply affect William Hulme; in later life he was determined to make some charitable provision for young boys.

William died in 1691 leaving an enormous philanthropic bequest, and was buried in Hulme Chapel of the Collegiate Church in Manchester, which had been largely built by his ancestors.

In his will William left provision for the foundation of 'exhibitions' or grants for four students to study for Bachelor of Arts degrees at Brasenose College. The income from this charity was originally £64 a year which came from rents and dues on William's many outlying properties at Heaton Norris, Denton, Ashton-under-Lyne, Reddish, Harwood, in Bolton, and in Manchester.

Over the years, with the growth of Manchester, the value and income from the original Hulme estate grew to such an extent that it became necessary on several occasions to change the scope of his bequest by Act of Parliament. In1881, the Trustees of the charity were empowered to build schools in Manchester, Oldham and Bury.

The Trustees also founded a Hall of Residence for students at Manchester University, made annual grants to the University itself, and to the Manchester High School for Girls. The exhibitions at Brasenose College were increased from four to twenty.

In 1881, the Trustees agreed to build a new school in Manchester. A site for it was bought off Alexandra Road, between Alexandra Park and Wilbraham Road. At that time, Spring Bridge Road was nothing more than a dirty lane petering out on the school site.

The new school was designed to accommodate 400 boys, with ample space for playgrounds, gymnasium and cricket fields. A headmaster, Mr Joseph Hall, was appointed on an annual salary of £150, plus a capitation fee of £2 for every boy admitted to the school.

The school opened on 26 January, 1887, with sixty-four boys. One Bernard Muth claimed to be the first pupil to step over the threshold. His devotion to the school would be evidenced by the fact that one of his last appearances at the school, before his death in 1965 at the age of 88, was when he played alongside his grandson in the school orchestra.

Few would ever forget the school's Latin motto 'Fide sed cui vide' - a punning witticism on the founder's name – 'Trust, but in whom take care'.

And if the motto were an insufficient reminder of whose bounty was ultimately behind the school's existence there was also the school prayer:

Top, facing page: William Hulme's Grammar School, circa 1920. *Bottom left, facing page:* The first class in 1887. *Above left:* An early twentieth century photograph of the school band. *Above:* The School Hall in the 1920s. *Below:* Chemistry lesson in 1927.

sporting events and academic triumphs. Laughter and tears; friends made for life.

Modern languages have become increasingly important in the present era, and William Hulme's is at the forefront of language teaching. In 2005 a brand new state-of-the-art digital language laboratory was opened at the school by an Old Hulmeian, Ivan Lewis MP, Economic Secretary to the Treasury.

The Member of Parliament was however far from being the only prominent visitor to the school in 2005. On Friday, 13 May, the school hosted a visit by their Royal Highnesses the Earl and Countess of Wessex. Also visiting the school were the Lord Mayor and Mayoress of Manchester, the Vice- Lord Lieutenant, the High Sheriff and local MP Sir Gerald Kaufman.

"O Lord, the resurrection and the life of them that believe, to be praised as well as those that live as in those that are departed: we give thee thanks for William Hulme, of whose bounty this school was founded and endowed, for William Roberts, Edward Donner and others our benefactors, past and present, by whose beneficence we are here maintained for the further attaining of Godliness and learning: beseeching thee to grant that we, well using to thy glory these Thy gifts, may rise again to eternal life with those that are departed in the faith of Christ: through Christ our Lord. Amen."

Down the many decades since the school first opened its doors thousands upon thousands of pupils have received their education at 'William Hulme' taking away with them at the end of their schooldays not only well earned examination certificates but also memories which last a lifetime.

No-one and nothing can ever erase those memories: teachers loved or hated, school dinners, ink wells and blotting paper; the smells of chalk dust and changing rooms; bad things such as the cane, and good things such as

William Hulme's Grammar School has been a city academy since 2007, and its ethos of high academic standards and extensive extra-curricular participation remains strong.

The Manchester Evening News recently reported that it is the most popular primary and secondary school in the whole of

time of writing there are two exceptional female athletes in Year 8, whilst two Year 10 boys are on Manchester City's books, and one Year 9 student trains regularly with Manchester United.

The Duke of Edinburgh scheme is incredibly popular, and approximately 20% of all students aged 15 and upwards are involved in some way with it. The Combined Cadet Force remains very strong under the leadership of Matthew Jones, and the most recent Biennial Review report was exceptional. Particular note was made of the confidence of the school's cadets and their ethnic and social diversity.

Greater Manchester. The school has a higher ratio of first choice applications for a place than any of the Trafford grammar schools.

Success has also attracted the attention of the national press, with the Daily Telegraph featuring the school in its lead article on admissions. 'William Hulme's' strong reputation is rooted in continued academic success. In 2011, 9 out of 10 students gained at least 5 good GCSE's with English and Mathematics and nearly 40% qualifying for the English Baccalaureate (GCSE passes in English, Maths, two Science subjects, a modern foreign language and History or Geography).

The school is also making good progress at A Level with 60% of students gaining A*-B grades, and the curriculum remains academic and challenging. One student gained a place to read Economics at Emanuel College, Cambridge, in October 2011. She had just completed a gap year trip to India where she visited William Hulme's 'link school', Toc-H, in Kerala.

Extra-curricular life of the school remains vibrant. There are a wide range of activities available after school each day. On average over 150 students play sport every evening, and Saturday sports are still an important feature of school life. At the

Meanwhile, the best of modern developments in education are being embraced. All classrooms are equipped with interactive whiteboards that help bring lessons to life and Old Hulmeians are encouraged to come into school and share the secrets of their successful careers with the current generation of students. The school, its staff and its pupils, are looking forward to the future, and continue to aim to make William Hulme's the best school in the Greater Manchester region.

Top left, facing page: A bird's eye view of the School and playing fields in the mid-1920s. *Centre, facing page:* Early study. *Above left:* The latest new build at the school - extension of the Donner Block. *Above:* Mr Peter Mulholland, Principal, 2012. *Below:* School photograph, 2011.

Waters MS Technologies Centre/Micromass UK Ltd
Solving the Mystery of Molecules

How do you test medicines to ensure that they are not counterfeit? How do you test soil, water and food for pollutants, or industrial chemicals for purity?

The magic of mass spectrometry is the answer. And when it comes to mass spectrometry the best magicians in the business are to be found in the North West of England at Micromass UK Ltd., now the Waters MS Technologies Centre, a company based in Floats Road, Wythenshawe.

Waters is making a significant investment in the future of Mass Spectrometry with plans to build a new Mass Spectrometry Headquarters in Wilmslow, Cheshire. The facility will be complete in late 2013 and has been designed to accelerate the rate of innovation and provide an inspiring environment for Waters employees and our customers.

Mass spectrometry is a means of analysing the tiniest amounts of substances to see what they are made up of at the atomic level. And it is no coincidence that Manchester should be at the cutting edge of such applied science.

In 1808, John Dalton, a Manchester Quaker schoolmaster and self-educated chemist, published his atomic theory in a book, his 'New System of Chemical Philosophy'. The theory was derived from, and rested upon, the observation that elements combine in fixed proportions according to their weights. John Dalton Street in Manchester was named in his honour.

Dalton was the first scientist to use experimental evidence to support the hypothesis that all element are made up of tiny, invisible, indivisible and unalterable atoms, each exactly the same as all other atoms of the same element, and each of which has a weight which could be calculated as a fixed multiple of the weight of an atom of hydrogen, the lightest element.

Almost a century later another Mancunian showed part of Dalton's picture of atoms to be not quite true. Sir Joseph John Thomson was born in Cheetham Hill, Manchester, and educated at Owens College before going to Cambridge in 1876. He subsequently became director of the famous Cavendish Laboratory in 1884. Thomson would claim the honour of being the man who discovered the electron, the first known sub-atomic particle.

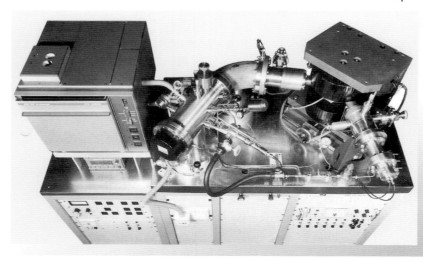

In 1904 Thomson built an apparatus which allowed streams of electrically charged atoms and similarly charged molecules (collectively known as ions) to be separated according to their mass. This was in effect the very first mass spectrometer, and in 1912 would famously lead to the discovery of the existence of isotopes –

Top left: *Robert Craig, founder of VG Micromass in 1968.* ***Above:*** *Alf Monks and Norman Lynaugh standing next to an early mass spectrometer.* ***Left:*** *A view of the Micromass 70-70 high resolution mass spectrometer, the first new product developed in Altrincham in 1975 .*

slightly different versions of atoms of the same element. The mass spectrograph subsequently developed by one of Thomson's students in the 1920s, Nobel Prize-winner, Francis Aston, allowed the mass, or weight, of atoms and molecules to be measured. J J Thomson himself deservedly received the 1906 Nobel Prize for Physics, and a knighthood in 1908. On his death in 1940, on the eve of the Battle of Britain, such was Thomson's fame that he would be buried in Westminster Abbey near the remains of Isaac Newton.

By the time of World War II all the isotopes of naturally occurring elements had been discovered and measured using mass spectrometry.

During the war, the research department of Metropolitan Vickers (MV) Electrical Company, at Manchester's Trafford Park, a company already experienced in vacuum engineering, built mass spectrometers for the United Kingdom Department of Scientific and Industrial Research as part of the development of the first atomic weapons.

Following the end of the Second World War the research department at Metropolitan Vickers continued to manufacture mass spectrometers for use in the analysis and identification of organic and inorganic substances. The earliest instruments made went to universities and petroleum companies.

The team at the MV research department worked, under Robert Craig, on the design and development of high-resolution mass spectrometers. In 1960 Metropolitan Vickers merged with other companies to form Associated Electrical Industries (AEI) and during the next decade became a world leader in the supply of high-resolution mass spectrometers.

In 1968, Robert Craig, foreseeing an unsettled future at AEI following a takeover by GEC, moved to Vacuum Generators (VG) in East Grinstead. Vacuum Generators had been formed in 1962 by Bernard Eastwell and colleagues to manufacture vacuum components. An embryonic mass spectrometer manufacturing programme was launched by Robert Craig and the early instruments were sufficiently successful to encourage the formation of VG Micromass Ltd, which in 1969, with a total of seven staff, moved to Winsford, in Cheshire, near to Manchester.

Above: An aerial view of Floats Road, Wythenshawe, factory opened in 1981. *Below:* A group of instruments in development at Floats Road, Wythenshawe, in 1985. The picture shows Peter Bott, now the Projects Program Manager, in the foreground working on a ZAB-4F - a tandem magnetic sector mass spectrometer and at the time the world's largest commercial mass spectrometer.

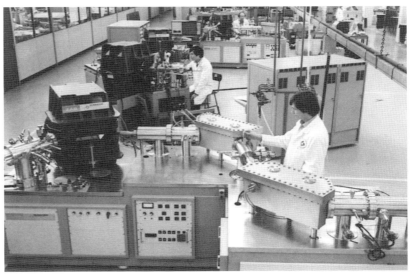

In December 1973, VG Micromass was split into several new companies, and two of them, VG Organic and VG Data Systems moved to Broadheath, Altrincham, under the management of Brian Green. The rationale behind the split was Bernard Eastwell's 'Christmas Card Principle' – most people send Christmas cards to 50-100 people, a number which represents a natural maximum of the number of people who can really get to know each other in a company and work together as a team.

VG Organic developed its first high-resolution mass spectrometer, the Micromass 70-70, in 1974. The first instrument was delivered to Oxford University in 1975 and was in use until 1997 when it was decommissioned and presented to the Manchester Museum of Technology.

During the 1980s, VG Organic and VG Datasystems was further split up to become VG Analytical, VG Masslab, VG Tritech and VG Biotech – each company selling different types of mass spectrometer to different but commonly overlapping markets.

In that same decade, Brian Green, who managed VG Organic when it was first established in Altrincham back in 1973, was awarded the OBE in recognition of his contribution to mass spectrometry technology. In 2010, Robert Bateman, former Technical Director, received an MBE in recognition of his services to science.

In 1986, the company won the Queen's Award for Exports and the following year the Queen's Award for Technology.

In 1991, the VG Group of Companies, by now owned by British American Tobacco (BAT), was sold to Fisons plc. Four years

Above: A view of instruments at various stages of assembly in the workshop at Floats road, Wythenshawe, 1985.

later in 1995 Fisons, the then troubled pharmaceutical company, decided to divest itself of its scientific instrument businesses. As a consequence the Manchester-based mass spectrometry companies (VG Analytical, VG BioTech and VG IsoTech) were acquired in 1996 by a management team led by Norman Lynaugh to become the newly constituted Micromass (UK) Ltd. At the outset Micromass employed some 250 people at its two sites: Broadheath, Altrincham, and Floats Road, Wythenshawe. By 2001, the number of employees in Manchester had swollen to 350 and Micromass opened a third site at Atlas Park, Simonsway, Wythenshawe. Today, Micromass employs more than 500 people in the Manchester area.

In 1997, the Waters Corporation, a US-based company with headquarters in Milford near Boston, Massachusetts, acquired Micromass.

Since 1958, Waters Corporation has been in the business of making analytical instruments that assist scientists in reaching their scientific goals. Whether at work discovering new pharmaceuticals, inventing new and more effective ways to treat diseases, assuring the safety of the world's food and drinking water supplies, monitoring and controlling pollution, or conserving the world's greatest art treasures, scientists worldwide rely on Waters liquid chromatography and mass spectrometry products.

In business for over 50 years, Waters is now one of largest companies in the analytical instruments industry, supporting scientists working in the world's 100,000 laboratories.

Waters Corporation is a world leader in the supply of liquid chromatography equipment. Liquid chromatography and mass spectrometry complement each other perfectly: a complex mixture may first be separated into its constituent parts and each component may be analysed and identified by the mass spectrometer as it 'elutes' or leaches out from the chromatograph.

In 2000, Micromass won two Queen's Awards, one for International Trade and one for Innovation. These awards were a consequence of the development of the Q-TOF mass spectrometer, a novel

industry. They are used primarily in the analysis of chemicals and biochemicals and have applications in the chemical, pharmaceutical, biotechnology and petroleum industries, in the life sciences and in environmental monitoring.

Two hundred years on since John Dalton developed his atomic theory it's thanks to firms like Micromass that the words 'science' and Manchester still remain inextricably linked.

tandem quadrupole 'time-of-flight' mass spectrometer that allows detection and identification of less than a pico-gram of a substance. A pico-gram is a millionth of a millionth of a gram, not only too small to be seen with the naked eye but almost too small even to imagine.

In 2006, Waters introduced a new instrument that not only allows the mass of molecules to be measured but also their shape and size. This instrument, developed by Micromass in Manchester, is the world's first commercial mass spectrometer to provide this capability.

Micromass is now primarily engaged in the business of developing and researching novel and leading-edge mass spectrometry instrumentation. The company is also engaged in the design, engineering and manufacturing of mass spectrometers for distribution through the Waters network. The instruments are sold throughout the world to universities, government research institutes, contract laboratories and to

Top left: *Brian Green being congratulated by Barry Mulady, then Managing Director of VG Analytical, for being awarded the OBE in 1985. Other Directors of the company are standing in the background, including Alf Monks and Norman Lynaugh (far right).* **Above:** *Bob Bordoli, then Managing Director of VG Analytical, receiving the Queen's Award in 1987 from the Lord Lieutenant of Manchester, employees raise a glass in the background.* **Below:** *Waters' new Mass Spectrometry Headquarters in Wilmslow, Cheshire, due to open in 2013.*

JW Lees - Be Yourself

As Shakespeare wrote in Hamlet, 'This above all: to thine own self be true'. Four hundred years later actress Judy Garland had a similar philosophy in mind when she advised "Always be a first-rate version of yourself, instead of a second-rate version of somebody else".

In 21st century Manchester local brewers JW Lees used fewer words when they adopted the slogan 'Be Yourself'.

The name of JW Lees may not be quite so well known around the world as Shakespeare or Judy Garland, but here in the North West the family firm's claim to fame is undisputed.

In 1828, retired cotton manufacturer John Lees had a twinkle in his eye. Or maybe he'd had a bad pint and wanted to get things right. He bought some land at Middleton Junction, started brewing and built Greengate Brewery, from where the company still operates.

John Lees' timing was immaculate. This was an age in which working men would drink up to twelve pints a day, women a little less and even the kids got in on the act. This wasn't because

water was considered a waste of throat-time – although there was a bit of that - but because you might catch something extremely nasty from it like cholera.

At the same time Manchester was becoming the workshop of the world and expanding rapidly. When demand meets quality at the right price you get success.

In 1876 John Lees' grandson, John William, took sole control of the Brewery and changed the name to JW Lees & Co. He didn't just keep his nose stuck in a mash tun either, finding time to become Mayor of Middleton twice.

JW Lees is one of the few remaining independent family brewers in the UK. It's got great beers and great pubs. It's even got a top-notch wine company called Willoughby's. This has been around in Manchester since 1850, almost as long as JW Lees, and is a business

Above: Founder, John Lees. Below: An early aerial illustration of Greengate Brewery, home of JW Lees for nearly two hundred years.

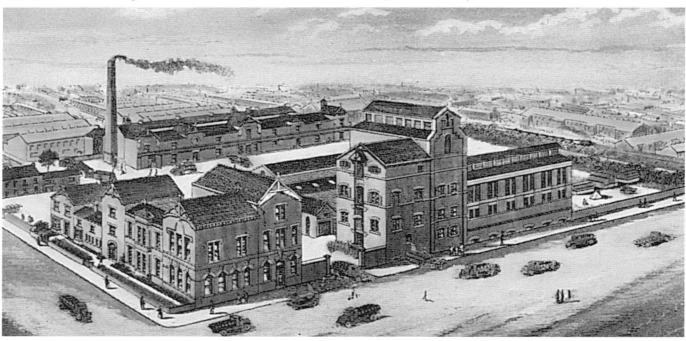

The JW Lees brewery has achieved national recognition. In 2003 HRH Prince Charles, The Prince of Wales, visited to celebrate the brewery's 175th anniversary, and in June 2004, Greengate Brewery was included in the television show Most Haunted.

During the 19th century several workmen died as the result of the sinking of the brewery well. In the 1930s, the supervisor was missing for several days until his body was recovered at the bottom of the same well.

All reports of hauntings are from those that actually worked at the brewery and some still working there today. Some of the apparitions include a woman sitting at the JW Lees boardroom table with her back up against the table, a lady wearing a long, brown dress walking into the kitchen through the staff door, and in the brew house, a figure in a white cloak has been seen several times.

One night watchman claims to have been hit across the face by someone as he passed by the boardroom. He was so frightened, he waited outside until other staff members arrived at 6am.

Another staff member, while eating lunch alone, felt as if someone else entered the room and was standing behind her. When she looked around, there was no one in sight.

that manages to be both old fashioned and cutting edge – but in the end they're just being true to themsleves.

Based in Middleton, the family business employs just over 1,000 people, 140 at the brewery and site in Middleton Junction and over 800 in its 30 managed pubs, as well as letting a further 142 tied pubs to self-employed tenants.

Cask beer is at the heart of JW Lees and the firm brews six cask ales as well as three lagers, three smooth beers and eight limited edition seasonal cask ales which are available at different times of the year. Its permanent brands are JW Lees Bitter, first brewed in 1828, John Willie's Premium Ale, Coronation Street Premium Ale (brewed under licence from ITV), Brewer's Dark, Moonraker, Dark Smooth, Extra Smooth, Greengate Smooth and Golden Original Lager. These days the company also has the sole UK distribution rights for Bohemia Regent Premium Lager from the Czech Republic.

JW Lees has been passed down the generations and today is in its sixth generation. In the early 1990s, William, Simon, Michael and Christina Lees-Jones joined fifth generation Richard and Christopher who, between them, have clocked up over 100 years' service at JW Lees. Richard joined the business in 1957 and Chrstopher in 1960. And there are definitely no plans for JW Lees to sell out to one of the bigger breweries.

Top left: Where and when it all began, Greengate Brewery in 1828. Above: A 1959 L.S Lowry sketch of Greengate Brewery. Below: A 1970s lorry all decked out for the local carnival.

In 2007, JW Lees launched an advertising campaign named 'Be Yourself'. The aim of the campaign is to acknowledge the traditional Northern roots of the family-owned brewery.

The campaign also highlights the fact that JW Lees real ales are brewed to the strictest purity standards, and that the company has invested in the pubs that make up its estate. In 2008, JW Lees Bitter, which has been brewed since 1828, won a silver award from CAMRA in the bitter category. Subsequently, the pubs were being recognised for their standards, with The Tandle Hill Tavern, Royton winning Pub of the Year at the 2007 Manchester Food and Drink Awards.

In November 2007, JW Lees launched the 'Grip Glass'. This is essentially a beer glass with grooves designed to fit into your hand, and it is available in most of JW Lees' pubs. Grip Glasses are also available for purchase from JW Lees.

To celebrate the 50th Anniversary of Coronation Street, JW Lees signed an advertising deal with ITV to produce a real ale bearing the famous soap opera's name. The ale can be bought in draft and bottles at JW Lees' public houses, and can also be purchased in bottles directly from JW Lees and local supermarkets around the Manchester area.

Meanwhile, expansion continued when, in 2009, JW Lees bought ten new pubs from Punch Taverns in time for inclusion in the fifth of the brewery's now legendary Passport Trail competitions.

The brewery's Passport Trail competitions have been run in 1983, 1990, 1997, 2003 and 2010. The aim of the competition is to have a pint of JW Lees' beer (only ales, bitter or lager brewed by JW Lees) in every one of their

Top left: A scene from Coronation Street as Bet Lynch has a meeting with the Chairman of 'Newton & Ridley' Brewery. The scene was actually shot in JW Lees Boardroom.
Left: A beer pump clip for JW Lees Coronation Street Premium Ale, brewed to celebrate 50 years of the UK's original soap.
Bottom left and below: Prince Charles visits JW Lees in 2003 in celebration of the company's 175th Anniversary.

H.R.H. The Prince of Wales on a visit to J.W. Lees Greengate Brewery - 17th November 2003

participating public houses across the North West of England and North Wales. Customers can take part by picking up a pocket-sized passport at participating JW Lees pubs. The passport has every participating JW Lees pub listed and the aim is to have it stamped at each establishment. The trail runs for 12 months and there are prizes available for customers who reach 25, 50, 125 and 162 pubs visited. The main prize is a VIP after-hours party at Greengate Brewery, hosted by the head brewer and

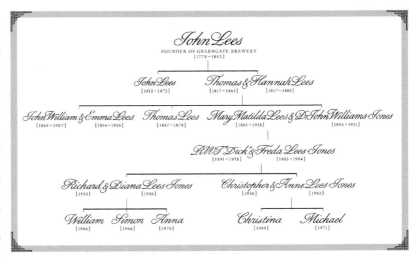

members of the Lees-Jones family. In 2010 almost 30 people completed the whole trail – one of them for the second time!

Still growing, the family company is always looking for new pubs, new customers and new people to join in – they say that they want to be the most exciting brewery in the North and that's just where they are going with their 'Be yourself' strategy.

According to the present generation of family owners:

"When we decided to face up to the challenges in the industry we took a long look in the mirror. The way forward was staring right back. It comes down to knowing where you've come from and where you're going. JW Lees is best when it keeps it real. No fuss, no flannel, no mission statements. We're a Northern brewery from Manchester England. That's why every aspect of our business, the people, the pubs, the beer, the food will measure up to our 'Be Yourself' standard.

We want great places for people to work in and play out. Places where people find excitement, but are comfortable too."

And if Shakespeare is not inspirational enough for the 21st century, Manchester's own Noel and Liam Gallagher, of classical quartet Oasis, made the point once more in a song called Supersonic – "You've got to be yourself, you can't be no-one else."

Spot on gentlemen. And mine's a pint.

Top left: JW Lees Bitter was awarded silver in bitter category by CAMRA at the 2008 British Beer Festival. In the picture is one of JW Lees Grip Glasses.. Top right: The JW Lees family tree. Above: A royal wedding beer pump clip for Middleton's which was brewed to commemorate the marriage of Prince William and Miss Catherine Middleton, 2011. Below: A modern view of Greengate Brewery.

Renold - The Chain of History

Renold plc is an international engineering group, producing a wide range of engineering products, operating in countries all around the world.

Based at Renold House, Styal Road, Wythenshawe, Renold plc is known globally as a supplier of quality transmission and conveyor chain as well as a range of high performance Gears and Couplings. Its founder was Hans Renold, 'The Father of the Chain Industry'.

Hans Renold was born on July 31st 1852, at Aarau, in Switzerland. Aarau was then a small mediaeval town. His father had a small bakery and restaurant under the town walls. The Renold family had been burghers of the town, probably since the Middle Ages.

Hans managed to get taken on by a local watchmaker in the school holidays. All his life he kept a watch which he bought for himself out of earnings from that early work. Later he attended the Polytechnic School at Zurich, and then had a brief period of military service.

As a young man of 20 Hans came to England in 1873. In Manchester he gained employment at Felber-Jucker, machinery exporters. After a short while he ventured into partnership with a gentleman named Calvert: together they exported machinery.

In 1879, Hans paid £300 for a small business in Salford, employing half-a-dozen people making rough chains for textile machinery. That same year J.K. Starley of Coventry brought out the 'safety bicycle' but the only chain that was available was the textile pin chain which quickly wore out. In 1880 Hans Renold designed and patented the bush roller chain, still in use today, which helped make the 'safety bicycle' a complete success. Due to Hans Renold the future of the bicycle was assured.

After 18 months Hans moved to larger premises in Brook Street, Manchester. The bicycle industry, however, developed so quickly it was impossible to produce chains fast enough. In 1889 Hans Renold started to build a six-storey building set back from Brook Street, Chorlton-on-Medlock. The building was known as 'Progress Works'.

To celebrate the opening of the new building in 1889 a party was given. In those days everything was much rougher and cruder, and to give a works party was an anxious experiment. The neighbourhood was an unsavoury one and drunkenness was commonplace.

The party, however, was a great success, though the men would not remove their caps when they danced, and a few people had to be tactfully persuaded to leave.

The party was the beginning of social life at the Works, which by 1910 finally blossomed into the Hans Renold Social Union.

Top: *Founder Hans Renold.* **Left, above and above inset small:** *Renold former premises: Brook Street Works, 1890 (left), Burnage Lane, 1905 (inset small) and Renold House, 1955.*

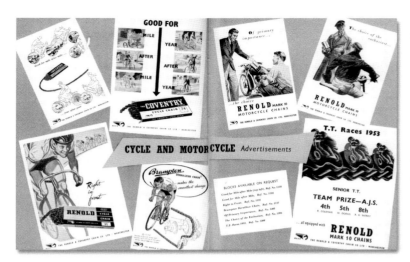

Hans soon realised that bicycle chains had other possibilities, and gradually evolved other types of chains for power transmission. He would work all evening over his drawing board at home. He introduced many new chain designs and patents. He also designed and manufactured machinery to make chain components and for their assembly.

Around 1895 Hans Renold started a Works Canteen. Another landmark was the introduction of the 48-hour week in 1896. There was a general demand throughout the engineering trade for shortening the hours of work, which at that time were 52 or more per week. Hans Renold, together with half-a-dozen other employers, believed that as much work could be done in 48 hours as in 52, and as a result he introduced the 48-hour week without a reduction of wages.

Hans Renold was also a keen enthusiast for standardisation of chain and associated products, and as early as 1897 he was instrumental in the introduction of Wheel (sprocket) Gauges Standards into the UK.

In 1898 Hans Renold made his first journey to America. The result was the introduction of Brown & Sharpe Autos into his Works. Hans Renold was also one of the first to introduce precision grinding into the UK as a production process.

By 1905 the business had outgrown the Brook Street site and Hans Renold purchased a large amount of land in Burnage. There he built his new factory, the 'Burnage Works' - together with his home, Priestnall Hey, which later became the site for the Hans Renold Social Union.

Although Burnage was then quite remote Hans Renold thought that he could best locate his new factory in the fresh air. He even had plans to start a farm on the site so that the Works would be self sufficient.

Top left: Early advertising of cycle and motorcycle chains. *Top right:* In 1954s 200-mile Daytona National Championship run the first five placed motorcycles were all equipped with Renold Mark 10 chains. **Centre:** A Renold service vehicle of 1954. **Left:** An example of Renold drive chains in the 1950s. **Above right and right:** Renold 1950s combined chain drive and gearbox (above right) and a gearbox (right).

The Works at Burnage remained until 1990 when the manufacturing facilities were moved to their present location in Bredbury, near Stockport.

Until 1903 the business had been a private one, with Hans Renold the sole proprietor. When the Company - Hans Renold Limited - was formed Hans presented blocks of shares to about a dozen leading employees.

From 1906 to 1914 the buildings at Burnage expanded bit by bit. The money came almost entirely from reinvested profits. Hans and his wife lived very simply: the needs of the business always came first.

During the 1914-1918 Great War the Works Committee movement began. The Hans Renold Company was one of a very few to welcome the Shop Steward movement.

Another notable achievement of Hans Renold included his adoption of a profit sharing scheme in 1922.

On 2nd May, 1943, after a period of failing health, Hans Renold passed away. It was the end of one era, but the beginning of another under the leadership of Hans' son Charles Renold. Charles evolved the company through his philosophy of direction, management and technology.

Renold established its first green-field manufacturing operation overseas in Melbourne, Australia, in 1947. This was followed by the establishment of other sales, and sometimes manufacturing, operations in Austria, Denmark, Malaysia, New Zealand, Singapore, South Africa, Sweden and Switzerland.

In 1948 Charles Renold was honoured with a knighthood for services to the cause of good management, and the development of humane and progressive ideals in industry.

In 1954 the company became Renold Chains Ltd and introduced its improved design of bi-planar chain.

Renold acquired Anchor Chain, Oldham in 1956. And now with the introduction of nuclear power at Calder Hall UK. Renold Chains Ltd. entered the Nuclear Age with the supply of control-rod lifting chains.

The Company was an innovator in the chain industry of progressive die tooling in the manufacture of chain plates. In 1959 chain plates for pitches between 1.0" and 1.5" were being produced by

Top left: A Renold exhibition stand at the Printing and Allied Trade Exhibition Olympia in 1955. ***Top Right:*** Sir Charles Renold. ***Left:*** The general machine section at Renold in 1963. ***Above:*** An early automobile engine test cell at Renold Works.

Solutions Chain

Transmission Chain

Conveyor Chain

Attachment Chain

Gears

Couplings

Renold acquired the Holset couplings business in Halifax in 1996, renaming it Renold Hi-Tec Couplings.

When clocks sounded the end of the 20th century and the start of the new millennium Renold staff knew something that most folk did not: the company had recently supplied a new chain for The Great Clock at the Palace of Westminster known more affectionately as 'Big Ben'.

In March 2000 Renold acquired Jeffrey Chain Corp., a leading manufacturer of industrial chain in the USA. Renold plc acquired Hangzhou Shanshui Chain Co. in China in 2007. In 2008 the Group acquired a controlling interest in L.G. Balakrishnan a chain manufacturing company in India.

this method. Smaller pitch chain plates had begun being produced by this process many years earlier.

In 1963 Renold acquired Arnold and Stolzenberg GmbH, one of the largest and longest-established chain manufacturers in Germany.

Further acquisitions brought more gearing, couplings, clutches, brakes, variable speed drives and various hydraulic products into the Group.

Now renamed Renold Ltd, in 1967 the Company developed a range of 'Non Lub' chains with 'sintered' bushes, soon to be followed by the press extrusion of bushes and rollers for transmission chain. In September that same year Sir Charles Renold sadly passed away.

Today Renold plc enjoys an annual turnover of some £190 million and employs around 2,500 people in more than 20 countries around the world.

Below left: A view of the Renold Styal Road site in the 1970s. Top left: A selection of Renold products. Left: Robert Davies, Chief Executive. Below: Renold have market-leading expertise across all the sectors in which they operate.

Renold began the cold extrusion of bushes for transmission chain using multi-station extruders in 1981. That same year a Renold chain was fitted to the Dartford Creek Barrier, a flood prevention scheme on the Thames.

Unsurprisingly Renold became the first chain company to obtain BS:5750, an accolade followed in the 21st century with ISO:14001.

Basic industries

Mining, oil, cement, steel

Construction

Off-road vehicles, lumber, major projects

Leisure

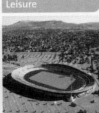

Theme parks, major events

Food

Palm oil, confectionery, beverages

Manufacturing

Original equipment manufacturers, printing

Transport

Shipping, freight handling, aerospace, mass transit

Infrastructure

Waste water plants, escalators, underground systems, power generation

RENOLDS

RRG Group
The North West's Leading Motor Dealership Group

The RRG Group has served the motoring needs of the North West for more than 45 years. There are nineteen dealerships across six franchises – Toyota, Lexus, Peugeot, Mazda, Suzuki and Kia – so there is a huge range of vehicles on offer. With two accident repair centres, RRG can provide a full range of services – car sales, service, parts, accessories and repairs.

Today, the RRG Group's head office is in the impressive Salford Quays dealership, but the business started life in a small garage in Bolton. The company was established by Michael Smyth in 1967, when he bought a garage on Radcliffe Road, with two petrol pumps and a workshop employing five mechanics.

Michael Smyth said, "We had two wooden huts and hand-cranked petrol pumps. My wife and kids would help out and we did quite well because we always had the 'customer first' ethic, long before it came into vogue."

Bill Tyldsley, who would later become vice-chairman, joined the company as a mechanic in 1968. RRG's first real venture into the motor retail industry came in 1971, when they became one of the first Toyota franchisees in the UK. Now, forty years later, RRG is the largest Toyota dealer group in Europe.

In 1972, Radcliffe Road Garage became a Limited Company and was employing fifteen people. This was a difficult time to be in the business; petrol prices were rising dramatically and there was a threat of petrol

Top left: Co-founder, Michael Smyth. **Above:** Bury Petrol Forecourt. **Below:** The Radcliffe Road site in the early years.

rationing due to action from OPEC. The UK economy was in turmoil and a three-day week was imposed. Yet for RRG, petrol sales continued to grow, especially when the company started to sell at discount prices.

"Supermarkets started discounting petrol and everyone was up in arms," said Michael Smyth, "then we started doing it and quickly we went from selling 400 gallons a month to 20,000 and then 60,000. It was incredible, really."

With the profits from this boost in sales, RRG purchased a carpet store and an old bus station, then knocked both down to build two new petrol stations.

Top: The Heywood site. *Above:* RRG Rochdale in the early 1990s. *Below left:* Bill Tyldsley. *Below:* Mr Smyth with Directors from Toyota GB.

Bill Tyldsley became a Director of the company in 1974. A year later the Elton Garage site in Bury was purchased. It was completely refurbished and opened as a Toyota dealership and petrol station in 1978. Petrol sales continued to rise, and the company found they needed more space for storing cars. A car preparation department was opened on Tonge Fold Industrial Estate, which was soon expanded to accommodate a new body shop complex.

Also in this period, a Peugeot franchise was added to the growing RRG Group. These dealerships operated under the Elton brand until 2007, when they were rebranded as RRG Peugeot.

The biggest change at RRG came in 2000, when the Marubeni Corporation approached Michael Smyth with an offer to buy the Group. Marubeni are one of the world's top 500 companies and one of the largest in Japan, where they were established in 1858.

In 1983 RRG took on another franchise – Ford – and a new dealership was established on Moorside Road, Swinton.

Throughout the 1980s and 1990s a number of petrol stations were purchased, among them were premises in Heywood and Irlam, but these were later sold so the company could focus on expanding its car dealerships.

RRG moved into the luxury car market in the 1990s when, once again, they became one of the first UK franchisees – this time for Lexus. Today, the Group operates three Lexus centres, in Manchester, Stockport and Bolton.

Michael Smyth said, "Out of the blue we were approached by one of the top companies in the world. They were Japanese, and so is Toyota, so for them it was a nice fit. They made us a very good offer and that's why we sold."

All RRG's staff were retained following the acquisition and Marubeni was keen for the Group to continue expanding the business.

In 2006 five additional dealerships were acquired representing Toyota, Lexus and a new franchise to the Group, Mazda.

Top left and top right: *The Elton Peugeot Centre, Bury, in 1997.* **Left and above:** *RRG Toyota Altrincham in the 1990s.*

The new sites were located in Stockport, Denton & Macclesfield. The Peugeot Centre on Bury New Road in Manchester also became a Mazda franchise in 2008.

2010 saw two new franchises introduced to the RRG Group: Suzuki was the first new addition in February, housed in a purpose-built facility next to the Group's existing Stockport centres.

Tony started work at RRG as a petrol pump attendant at the age of sixteen. He worked his way up and was General Manager at RRG's successful Bolton Toyota dealership before his move to Head Office.

The Group continues to grow: in 2011 RRG Mazda Rochdale was opened on Kingsway, and Suzuki Manchester opened in 2012.

Today, RRG Group employs a workforce of over 650 across nineteen dealerships in six franchises. Whatever your motoring needs, RRG Group's experienced and highly-qualified staff can provide you with all the products and services you require, from a huge range of manufacturers.

Kia became the second new franchise in June of that year, taking over the former Peugeot site in Bury to extend RRG's increasingly diverse portfolio.

In 2011 the management structure was streamlined and Arran Bangham and Tony Cliff were appointed Joint Managing Directors. Arran started in the financial side of the business in 1995 and has been involved in many of the most significant developments at RRG in the years since.

Above left: RRG's Suzuki Stockport showroom. *Above* The RRG Group's Flagship Salford Quays Toyota showroom and head office. *Bottom left:* The company's purpose-built Toyota premises on Bury New Road, Bolton. *Below:* Tony Cliff and Arran Bangham, joint managing directors.

Joseph Gleave & Son

The Journey so far: from Tool Maker to Industrial Supplies Specialist

Today Joseph Gleave & Son Ltd is a leading industrial supplies specialist that offers a diverse product range, distributed nationwide. Whether they need tools, consumables, safety & hygiene products or site equipment, 'Gleave' provides the goods and services to meet clients' specific requirements.

Now based in Chester Road, Stretford, the company is renowned for its extensive product range and technical expertise. With 180 years' experience within industry, a highly qualified team understands industrial supply requirements and proactively supports customers to provide a tailored range of products and services. The company is rooted in Manchester, with its origins going back to the reign of William IV.

The founder, Joseph Gleave, had been working for several years as a plane maker when in 1833 he formally started the company which today bears his name. He began trading as 'Wooden Plane Manufacturers and Dealers of Tools and Sheffield Cutlery'. All Gleave wooden planes were manufactured in the Gleave workshop based in Spear Street, Manchester, and were made from high quality beech wood dry cured for 20 years. Joseph also had retail and wholesale premises located at 120, Portland Street, Manchester. Such wooden planes, collectors' items today, had been used since antiquity, but their days were numbered. In 1859 Joseph retired and his son Joseph James Gleave took over the running of the company.

Top left: *Founder, Joseph Gleave.*
Right: *Joseph J Gleave, son of the founder.*
Below: *J. Gleave & Son 8 Oldham Street premises which they occupied from 1853-1913.*

In the mid-1860s, Leonard Bailey in the USA began producing a line of cast iron-bodied hand planes, the patents for which were later purchased by Stanley Rule & Level, now Stanley. The original Bailey designs were further evolved and added to by Justus Traut and others at Stanley Rule & Lever. The Bailey and Bedrock designs became the basis for most modern metal hand plane designs manufactured today.

Following the introduction of the highly successful metal-based plane, Gleave diversified to provide a range of tools including joiners' tools and garden tools. The second half of the 19th century was a time of remarkable growth and prosperity for Manchester, with demand for goods of all kinds growing almost daily. Gleave grasped the opportunities presented with alacrity.

Joseph James Gleave ran the business until 1892, but with no son to pass the business on to he asked his cousin John Shaw to take on the firm. Gleave now passes through the Shaw family name, with John Shaw passing the business onto his nephew Arthur John Shaw in 1919, who retired in 1985. After the Second World War the company participated in the Lend Lease programme set up by the Americans for the UK and rest of Europe to replenish

goods after the war. Gleave started to supply UK manufacturers with tools and machinery as part of that scheme. In the 1950s Gleave diversified again and became manufacturers of the Longford Grinder, with production based at Talbot Rd, Stretford, Manchester. This grinder was one of the first motorised whetstone grinding machines; popular with schools which used them to sharpen chisels and plane irons.

Top: *2a Piccadilly, home to Joseph Gleave & Son, circa 1920.* **Centre:** *Early Gleave products.* **Below:** *Workshop at Great Ancoats Street.*

Gleave promoted the Longford Grinder at educational exhibitions and began to build a reputation for high quality tools and machinery. The company started to supply education authorities, schools, colleges and universities with the grinder and a range of tools and other machinery. Customers included the Education Committees of Manchester, Cheshire, Durham, Leicestershire, Derbyshire, Cornwall and Essex.

In 1954 David Shaw, Arthur John Shaw's son joined the business and it was he who, in 1966, made a strategic decision to expand and opened a warehouse at Longford Trading Estate. The extra capacity enabled the company to stock both hand and machine tools to meet increasing demands from industry.

Following that expansion Gleave wanted to develop a strong customer base in industrial sectors, and so began to forge relationships. Good service and a wide product range enabled Gleave to set up divisional contracts which in time grew and grew. Gleave began to serve a wider region, providing industrial supplies to various branches or divisions of national companies such as British Aerospace, British Gas, BNFL, Central Electricity & Generating Board, ICI, Shell and Vauxhall Motors.

In 1975 Gleave moved to 995, Chester Road, Stretford, Manchester. This move enabled even more expansion of the machine tools side of the business. An economic downturn hit the UK in the 1980s, significantly reducing expenditure in education - a core sector Gleave had serviced for many years. Determined to survive and prosper, Gleave developed exporting opportunities and began to appoint agents abroad. Gleave was successful, winning tenders to provide industrial supplies to vocational institutions and universities as far away as Indonesia, Jordan, Malaysia, Sudan and Syria.

Top: A Gleave exhibition stand at Manchester's Corn Exchange in 1957. *Left:* From their purpose-built Distribution Centre Gleave operate an intelligent stock control and logistic system with the latest materials handling equipment, so all products are efficiently moved via a conveyor system. *Above:* Gleave warehouse and distribution centres totalling 45,000 sq ft from which 12,000 product lines are managed.

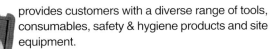

Major projects included equipping the Aleppo and Damascus Universities and Khartoum Power Station Training School. Most of those programmes were funded by the World Bank or the European Bank, and involved providing industrial supplies to the Middle East, Far East, Africa and the Caribbean.

John Shaw, the son of David Shaw, joined the business in 1980, and today holds the position of Managing Director.

In the Public Sector Gleave began to supply the Ministry of Defence with specific supplies of tools and other products. In 2001 Gleave was appointed Industrial Prime Vendor to the Ministry of Defence supplying a diverse product range including abrasives, adhesives, hand tools, pneumatic tools, tapes and sealants.

In the Private Sector businesses started to centralise purchasing operations and Gleave became one of the leading providers of industrial supplies - a position it still holds today. Amongst its customers are BT, Transco and British Gas.

Expansion continued and Gleave embarked on a major construction programme to develop a new Head Office and purpose-built Distribution Centre which was completed in May 2002. Today Gleave employs around 70 people, and still evolves and adapts to ever changing market opportunities. Developing strong links with a wide variety of manufacturers it

provides customers with a diverse range of tools, consumables, safety & hygiene products and site equipment.

"Gleave's longevity is due to sheer determination and our ability to adapt to an ever changing market. For 180 years we have had to diversify our product range and look for new and emerging opportunities, we've survived two depressions and have delivered industrial supplies on a worldwide basis," explains John Shaw.

"For a company to survive 180 years is astounding, to put it into perspective we are older than the telegraph (1837), the telephone (1876) and the light bulb (1879)."

So what does the future hold for Gleave? According to John Shaw: "We hope the next 180 years are as prosperous as the last. We are determined and extremely focused on our business strategies and our integrity to deliver quality products competitively. We are extremely proud of our strong heritage and strive to continue to deliver a personal service."

Top: *Examples of the company's storage and tool box sets.* **Left:** *Gleave Head Office, Stretford, Manchester.* **Above:** *David Shaw and son John Shaw.*

Withington Girls' School - A Century of Achievement

Withington Girls' School, in Wellington Road, Fallowfield, is a leading independent day school for girls aged 7 to 18, where some of the best academic results in the country are attained within a lively, happy and caring environment.

The School was founded in 1890 by a group of eminent Manchester families, including Mr C P Scott, the first editor of the Manchester Guardian, and Mr Henry Simon, of Simon Engineering fame, along with his wife Emily. Together with Miss Caroline Herford, Mrs Louise Lejeune and Dr Adolphus Ward, these visionary men and women determined to establish a school that would provide the same educational opportunities for their daughters as for their sons – not least in the sciences.

Number 16 Mauldeth Road was the School's first home. Though the fires smoked and the drains were seriously defective, the School thrived. By 1903 growing numbers meant that larger premises were needed.

The new building was on the edge of farmland on Wellington Road, then a mere a cart track. 'Woodlands', the core of the current building, had been built in 1888 by Mr L Pughe as an independent boys' school; it was bought for £3,000 and Mr Pughe moved his boys to North Wales.

An outbreak of sore throats in 1905 led not only to the School being closed for three weeks, but also to the first of the 'new'

buildings. Mrs Simon offered to buy a small Cottage Sanatorium which was erected on the north-west corner of the site. It remained there for over 30 years before being moved nearer to the School to become the Staff Room. Though seldom used for infectious ailments, the building proved extremely useful for cricket and hockey teas and for Saturday morning cookery classes.

The next major extension, built in 1913, cost £225 7s 11d; it now looks like part of the original building.

Electricity was installed in 1923, removing the anxiety before entertainments lest something should happen to the gas lighting in the gymnasium. The provision of a new gymnasium with an expensive pyengadu

(Burmese ironwood) floor was followed by a state-of-the-art Chemistry laboratory in 1934, reflecting the continuing commitment to the Founders' vision of a school where physical and scientific education, rarely offered with rigour to girls, formed part of a broad curriculum.

Four long-serving headmistresses ensured that Withington's development

Top: The School's earliest photograph dating from the late 1800s. **Centre left:** The first school building - 16 Mauldeth Road. **Above:** An early 1900s view of Woodlands. **Left:** A race for the finish line in this Withington Girls' sports day photograph of the 1920s.

The result is a community where pupils are enthusiastic learners who take full advantage of the impressive breadth of educational and personal opportunities. A-level and GCSE results consistently confirm the School's position as one of the top ten schools in the UK and the best performing school in the North of England.

kept pace with the times. They were Miss Margaret Grant (1908-1938), Miss M Elsbeth Bain (1938-1961), Miss Marjorie Hulme (1961-1985) and Mrs Margaret Kenyon (1986-2000). Under them the School prospered and its academic standards never wavered.

At the start of the new millennium, under the leadership of its Headmistress, Mrs Janet Pickering, Withington Girls' School reinforced its high reputation and standards. Today, led by Mrs Sue Marks, the School continues to excel in both its extra-curricular provision as well as academic results. The School values its links with the local Manchester community - many older pupils enjoying their experience of voluntary work with the elderly or the young in neighbouring schools and hospitals. Withington girls are also committed to raising funds for charities both close to home and further afield.

The girls thrive in a friendly and caring environment, and leave to take up their higher education places personally, socially and academically prepared for the next phase of their lives.

Despite its Victorian origins, Withington provides a wealth of opportunity for the young woman of the 21st century. The Founders would be proud of their legacy.

Top left: A view of the rear of the School and the newly erected Sanatorium in 1905. Above: Experimenting in a Chemistry lesson in the 1970s. Left: Girls in a Design Technology class. Below: Headmistress, Mrs Marks, with pupils, 2012.

In keeping with the wishes of its Founders, the School has remained relatively small, to allow for the individual development of each girl. With fewer than 100 girls in the Junior School and 560 in the Senior, the School retains a friendly, responsive environment which best encourages each girl to fulfil her whole potential. The School also benefits greatly from the cosmopolitan background which the City and University of Manchester have always provided. Girls from less financially advantaged backgrounds are not disadvantaged academically, with one-in-six students in the Senior School benefiting from a Bursary-funded place.

ACKNOWLEDGMENTS

The publishers would like to sincerely thank a number of individuals and organisations for their help and contribution to this publication.

Local Studies Department, City Library, Manchester

Getty Images

Aerial View of Belle Vue Gardens in 1930